The Best
AUSTRALIAN POETRY
2004

THE BEST AUSTRALIAN POETRY SERIES

The Best Australian Poetry 2003,
Guest Editor: Martin Duwell

The *Best*
AUSTRALIAN POETRY
2004

Guest Editor
ANTHONY LAWRENCE

Series Editors
BRONWYN LEA
MARTIN DUWELL

UQP

First published 2004 by University of Queensland Press
Box 6042, St Lucia, Queensland 4067 Australia

www.uqp.uq.edu.au

Typeset by University of Queensland Press
Printed in Australia by McPherson's Printing Group

Distributed in the USA and Canada by
International Specialized Book Services, Inc.,
5824 N.E. Hassalo Street, Portland, Oregon 97213-3640

This project has been assisted by
the Commonwealth Government through
the Australia Council, its arts funding
and advisory body.

Sponsored by the Queensland Office
of Arts and Cultural Development

This publication is proudly sponsored by The Josephine Ulrick
and Win Schubert Foundation for the Arts.

Cover painting by Anwen Keeling, *Obedience Isn't Everything*, 2003 Oil on
Canvas (61 x 91.5 cm) courtesy of the artist and Art Galleries Schubert

Cataloguing in Publication Data
National Library of Australia

The best Australian poetry 2004.
   1. Australian poetry — 21st century — Collections.
   I. Lawrence, Anthony, 1957–   . II. Duwell, Martin, 1948–   .
   III. Lea, Bronwyn, 1969–   .

ISBN 0 7022 3444 3

CONTENTS

Bronwyn Lea and Martin Duwell

Foreword

The Best Australian Poetry 2004 is the second of our projected
annual surveys of contemporary Australian poetry published in
literary journals and newspapers. We are encouraged by the
overwhelming reception of the inaugural edition, *The Best Aus-
tralian Poetry 2003*, (pre-sales made necessary a reprint before
the book was officially released) and this has given us confi-
dence in the future of the series. Already we can see the benefits
of a policy of engaging a different Guest Editor each year — this
year, Anthony Lawrence — in that this selection feels radically
different to last year's. Rather than attempting a magisterial
overview, we have always felt that the varied perspectives of
changing Guest Editors will make, in the long run, for a rich and
more accurate portrait of what is happening in poetry in Aus-
tralia. At the practical level, this second volume has enabled us
to think more carefully about those matters of policy which seem
commonsensical in the abstract but which, in practice, come
down to irritatingly minute decisions. Matters of nationality for
eligible poets comprise one set of thorny examples, as do the list
of journals from which the poems will be selected. In both cases,
we have reconsidered but decided to continue our policy of
including only poems by Australian citizens and residents pub-
lished in Australian print journals and newspapers. The former
generated problems when Lawrence's initial selection of the
'best forty poems' included a poem by an American poet who

had somehow slipped through our filter: jettisoning the poem and requesting a replacement caused some awkward last minute readjustments. In the case of the latter, we felt our decision was a bit harsh on journals such as *Antipodes* — the journal of the American Association for Australian Literary Studies — which has, for a number of years now, done a magnificent job of bringing Australian literature into the North American ambit and which, at the same time, continues to publish a number of fine Australian poems in each issue. But as well as celebrating Australian poets and poetry, we had decided at the outset to celebrate those journals and newspapers which, in the difficult climate of Australian culture with its attendant problems of lack of financial resources and lack of broad community support, nevertheless continue with a commitment to the poetry of Australia.

In a year in which Australia went to war, albeit as a small component of the 'Coalition of the Willing,' it is perhaps not surprising that one of the issues raised during 2003 involved poetry's commitment to the public sphere. The positions of poets, as always, covered a span. At one end is an essential, though sometimes despairing, quietism inevitably invoking Auden's 'poetry makes nothing happen: it survives / in the valley of its making,' though perhaps missing Auden's point that, although the overarching cultural and physical conditions do not change (Ireland remains mad and its weather remains terrible), poetry's survival as 'a way of happening, a mouth' is itself a cause for hope. At the other end is a belief in poetry's capacity to be at least a component of protest. In March 2003, a collection of poems by 119 Australian poets was delivered to Australia's Prime Minister as part of an international Day of Poetry Against the War. The poets included ten associated with this year's *Best Australian Poetry* anthology: Robert Adamson, Adam Aitken, Judith Beveridge, Peter Boyle, MTC Cronin, Anthony Lawrence, Emma Lew, Les Murray, Thomas Shapcott and Chris Wallace-Crabbe. Speaking on behalf of Australian poets against the war, Alison Croggon's comment that the collection was a 'flotilla of poems which matches [Australia's] military presence in the Middle-East — small, but symbolically significant' perhaps strikes the right note for poetry in its engagement with the world's macro-events: ambitious but realistic.

It is sad to have to record, in this introduction to our second volume, the passing of one of the contributors to the first volume. Norman Talbot, who died in January 2004, was a fine, if underrated, poet and a thoroughly distinctive voice in Australian poetry. His first two books, *Poems for a Female Universe* (1968) and its whimsically named sequel, *Son of a Female Universe* (1971), contain poems that one remembers fondly after more than thirty years. Talbot's prize-winning poem sequence, 'Seven New South Wales Sonnet-Forms,' is included in this volume, and it was our sad task to inform Lawrence who, tucked away in Hobart, had not heard news of Talbot's passing but had nonetheless selected this poem on merit. Another passing of importance was that of Clem Christesen, a Brisbane poet and prose writer who began *Meanjin Papers* as a small magazine in late 1940 in Brisbane. After the war the journal moved to Melbourne, contracted its name to *Meanjin*, and established itself as Australia's premier cultural journal in the post-war period.

As we've stated, one of the many aims of this series is to celebrate those journals, such as *Meanjin* and the new and impressive literary journal *Salt-lick New Poetry*, which continue to publish quality Australian poems, as well as to celebrate those editors who devote immense stretches of time and infinite energies to produce quality magazines. On a more coercive (though suitably muted) note, we hope that the series will also encourage poets to renew contact with these journals. While emerging poets derive immense support and confidence from publication in small magazines, established poets sometimes withdraw while preparing book-length manuscripts and contribute poems to magazines not as a matter of course, but only when asked. There is a certain irony in the fact that the Guest Editor of this volume did not appear in the inaugural issue, having published no poems in literary journals in 2002. While he did publish poems in journals in 2003, we are grateful that he agreed to forego possible inclusion in *The Best Australian Poetry 2004* and agreed to be its Guest Editor instead.

In a series of books, beginning with *Dreaming in Stone* (UQP, 1989) and now his most recent *The Sleep of a Learning Man* (Giramondo, 2004), Lawrence has established himself as one of Australia's pre-eminent poets with a passionate and distinctive voice celebrated for its muscular movement, kaleidoscopic vision, and musical complexity. Lawrence's poems and collections have won just about every prestigious poetry prize in Australia, including the Newcastle Poetry Prize (1997) and the Josephine Ulrick Poetry Prize (2001), as well as the Judith Wright Calanthe Poetry Prize (1991) and the New South Wales Premier's Kenneth Slessor Prize for Poetry (1996). His poetry is rightly admired by many for its exploration of the immense drama of the Australian landscape, capturing not only the harshness of rural life but also meditating on the intricate and startling details of native birds, fish and flora. But Lawrence is also intensely interested in the human animal and, in this aspect, his poems are often set into continual motion, converging and dispersing in a kinetically-charged human drama. It's perhaps not surprising, then, that the forty poems he has selected for this anthology contain not only many poems about animals — dogs, horses, birds, bats, fish and the platypus — but also many poems about love, romantic and familial, with all the violence and tenderness that these relationships incite and demand. There are poems too that explore the human at home in the body — a body that oozes, bleeds and aches, but one that also loves, desires and heals — as well as poems that are intensely interested in language, another of Lawrence's own interests, and in how poetry might effectively address the cerebral and political dimensions of creative life. Lawrence's selection is not only intelligent but also dramatic and flamboyant, revealing an unquenchable and quirky passion for life immersed in the magnificent clutter of lived reality.

———

During the proofing of this introduction we received word of the death of Bruce Beaver at the age of seventy-six. He was one of Australia's greatest poets, an indefatigable writer and a great celebrator and lamenter. His most admired book was his fourth, *Letters to Live Poets*, published in 1969, but the volumes that followed it — *Lauds and Plaints* and *Odes and Days*, as well as the volumes that followed these books — are major contributions to Australian poetry. Beaver showed Australian poets how it was possible to be wide-ranging and international in one's reading and one's concerns while writing in a way that seems absolutely Australian. He was always concerned with poets and his two totemic poets were Po Chu-I (whose unstoppable ability to turn life into poetry was something he admired) and Rilke. One of the best poems in Beaver's first book, *Under the Bridge* (1961), is 'Remembering Golden Bells … and Po Chu-I,' which retells the story of the Chinese poet's loss of his little daughter, Golden Bells. It seems fitting that in one of his final poems — from his posthumous collection *The Long Game and Other Poems* (UQP, 2005) — Beaver recalls his Chinese mentor:

LATE AFTERNOON

A last radiance of sunlight
illuminates an empty chair, an empty couch.
Visitors are few and when they come
I don't wish them away
but do hope they won't stay too long
for my closest friends are books and blank paper.
My fingers itch for the pen and later
my eyes focus on the pages of others.
It's understandable: I'm in my seventies
and though the days moving into summers
are growing longer, my years are growing shorter.
Like Po Chu-I, I have been away from the Capital
a long time; though I have not lost any children
I watch the faces of acquaintances
and see in them a lost child here and there.
Surely parenthood is a vocation
like poetry, unlike poetry.

GUEST EDITOR

ANTHONY LAWRENCE

Anthony Lawrence was born in Tamworth, New South Wales, in 1957. He left school at sixteen, working first as a jackeroo and then travelling for several years before returning to New South Wales to work as a teacher and writer. It was while working as a fisherman in Western Australia that he secured a literary fellowship which enabled him to devote time to writing poetry. Over time, his poems have appeared in many Australian and international literary magazines. His books include *The Sleep of a Learning Man* (Giramondo, 2004); *Skinned by Light: Poems 1989-2002* (UQP, 2002); *The Viewfinder* (UQP, 1997); *The Darkwood Aquarium* (Penguin, 1993); *Three Days Out of Tidal Town* (Hale & Iremonger, 1992); *Dreaming in Stone* (Angus & Robertson, 1989); and the novel *In the Half Light* (Picador, 2000).

Lawrence is the recipient of a Senior Fellowship from the Australia Council — one of the most prestigious funding awards a writer can be accorded in Australia — and has won numerous awards for his poetry, including the inaugural Judith Wright Calanthe Award; the Harri Jones Memorial Award; the Gwen Harwood Memorial Prize; the Josephine Ulrick Poetry Prize; the NSW Premier's Award; and the Newcastle Poetry Prize.

The *Oxford Companion to Australian Literature* describes his poetry as narrative with a strong lyrical vein, and the Austlit Gateway entry for him is extensive: 'his poetry explores many aspects of Australian landscape, capturing the harshness of rural life, but also meditating on the minute and beautiful details of native birds, fish and animals.' Currently, a selection of his work is being translated into German.

He lives in Hobart with his son Cormac.

ANTHONY LAWRENCE

INTRODUCTION

During an episode of *The Addams Family*, Don Rickles and someone who looked like Christopher Walken *sans* the menace, were attempting to con the family out of their fortune. It was Christmas. Typically, Gomez Addams was blissfully unaware of the subterfuge, smoking his cigar and gleefully showing his guests around. Then he decided, it being Christmas, that he would read the two men a poem. He sat them in hard-backed chairs in the parlour. Before he began, Don Rickles turned to his friend and said, 'Poetry? I'd rather be back in prison.'

It seems the scriptwriter was broadcasting the general attitude to poetry on the day: something to be avoided, something difficult and, in this case, sentimental and quietly confrontational. I want to see poetry on Reality TV. I want someone on a show like *Big Brother* or *Survivor* to read a poem; one they've written or one from a book they couldn't bear to leave at home. Imagine. Somewhere in a lull between prescriptive, banal conversations in a lounge room or on the beach, someone calls for a little quiet and reads Michael Dransfield's 'Minstrel.' Dream on.

In our culture we've never known soccer stadiums packed with poetry-lovers listening to ghazals; we're not used to hearing the local grocer quote from Heaney or Larkin, Adamson or Slessor. Though here's a story: when I first came to Fern Tree, on the lower-slopes of Mount Wellington, I pulled into the local, independently-run garage for petrol. Blues was leaking from the back of the shop. Neville, the proprietor, having a keen eye for blow-ins, asked me where I was living and what I did for that living. When I told him I was writing poetry, he ran off into the blues and metallic workshop sounds, vanished through the folds of dark blue curtains and returned with a copy of John Forbes' *Collected Poems*, which he thrust at me, saying, 'Now this man is wonderful.'

In Rome, 1994, during a six-month residency, I bought the *Sunday Independent* and found, in the weekend magazine, a four-page feature article on contemporary British poetry. There were colour photographs and lengthy accompanying details — some anecdotal, largely biographical — of Simon Armitage, Glyn Maxwell, Kate Clanchy, Carol Anne Duffy, Kathleen Jamie, Don Paterson and Lavinia Greenlaw. Here was a public showcasing of poetry. The article took centre stage in a glossy magazine. The general public were being introduced to a new generation of relatively young poets, with examples of their work. It was an important statement: *Poetry matters. Here are some exciting, innovative voices.*

While poetry in Australia is not given the same space or kudos in our print media, it's never been more alive, both in terms of what's being written and performed, and in the number of people actively involving themselves in its appearance, in its many forms. That the mainstream publishers have all but turned their backs on poetry has had no impact on what's emerging. The small presses have been producing some amazing books by new, young poets and established, older writers. And the number of poems being published in the magazines and journals is astounding. Working my way through the hefty stack of folders containing what was published throughout 2003, I was surprised and delighted by what I found.

Stylistically, things have changed dramatically in the last few years. There's been an interesting follow-on from the Language poetry that left an indelible mark on some poets. It seems that the work of Americans like Charles Bernstein, Lyn Hejinian, Bernadette Mayer and Ron Silliman, and their influence on some Australian poets has been aligned with a lyrical, accessible vernacular, so that a poem becomes an investigation of, and a testing-ground for, both syntax and form. The reader is welcomed into the work and, while being challenged, is simultaneously guided — not via code or against closure — but by the irresponsibility of imagination, coupled with fine craft. The work of Ted Nielsen comes to mind. His wonderful poem 'Pax Romana' knocked me out with its fusion of tight, pacey lines thick with original images, glimpsed, it seems, through flashing windows. I can hear John Forbes in the distance, talking quietly yet passionately about line-breaks, exhaustion and travel.

This anthology opens with Robert Adamson's 'Flag-Tailed Bird of Paradise,' a stunning poem that reveals Adamson's ability to combine the natural world with any number of important, political, social themes, and to make of that combination a startling, arresting marriage of language and rhythms. Here, Adamson places these rare, white-tailed birds into the recent Iraq war, but not before he's traced their passage from the Pacific Islands to Arabia. The journey takes twenty-one spellbinding, evocative lines. Judith Beveridge's 'Appaloosa' is a poem about language but also one which goes to the heart of her subject matter. It flows like an incantation, and by the end of it the poem reeks of all things equine.

I'm aware that my choices cover a wide range of styles and writing experience. And while this was certainly not intentional, I'm thrilled that such a disparate list has emerged. I'm happy to include the work of poets like Liam Ferney and Lidija Cvetkovic, among others. Cvetkovic's poems have been appearing in journals for some time now, and her first book, *War Is Not the Season for Figs*, due out this year from University of Queensland Press, will be a cause for celebration. One of the most exciting things to emerge while reading through these poems was to encounter, again, Luke Davies' extraordinary 'Totem Poem.' When I first read it in *Heat*, I was somewhat distracted by all things domestic. Now, I realise what a major poem it is. Davies has written a long, meditative love poem, set against and within an ever-changing emotional and physical landscape. Pollen and wind adhere to, and groom the undercurrents and surface eddies of, this ambitious work. When I first read Luke Davies' poetry, I had a sense that here was a poet to watch out for. Now he's well and truly arrived, with confidence, disarming grace and tenderness.

Mark Strand wrote: 'For some of us, the less said about the way we do things the better. And I for one am not even sure that I have a recognisable way of doing things, or if I did that I could talk about it.' While I agree with him, I think it's important to discuss, albeit briefly, what this guest editorial has meant to me. It's refocussed my commitment to finding and reading new work by new poets; it's challenged my ideas on where current trends in poetry lie, and how they've been shaped; and it's driven me back to my own work, armed with a fresh, raw energy. All the poets represented here made their poems in solitude, or close to it, and I'd hazard a guess that most of these poems defined their own terms, carved their own passage, announced their departures and arrivals, and surprised their makers right up to the end. I'm reminded of Archie Ammons, who talked of how the best poetry creates a sense of us being inside our bodies while remaining outside of ourselves. This anthology has forty poems that reveal real craft, risk-taking that never overreaches itself, and most importantly, they offer us amazing new ways to see the world. If there is still a deep-rooted fear that poetry — by its very nature, by what it has become, and by what readers of it experienced in school — is too difficult to apprehend, then it is my hope that this anthology will go some way to repair the rift between poetry and readers. Some of the poems here are challenging but all of them — in their idiosyncratic and life-affirming ways — are, given a chance, rewarding.

ROBERT ADAMSON

FLAG-TAILED BIRD OF PARADISE

(George W. Bush instructed 'the enemy' to hold up white flags and stand twenty metres away from their tanks, promising that if they did, they would be spared)

Thought to be extinct, they are
appearing through the red mist, their white tails
waving at blunt helicopters splattering
the earth. These creatures
from paradise play dead when attacked —
they freeze, clamped to a branch,
the tiny flags of their tails
barely shimmering in broken sunlight.
They once lived in jungles
on islands in the Pacific, but haven't
been found dead there since 1958.
Some escaped to Arabia: sold to collectors
and bred in captivity, they were
taken up by zoos, kept in palaces
and inbred. Flunkies fed them
and sultans hovered about them, marvelling
at how they became extraordinary in their deformities,
their cream-coloured plumage shot

through with pale, beautiful rainbows,
their eyes enormous, pink, their tail-flags heavy —
almost too heavy to hold up, but not theirs to withhold.

Meanjin

ADAM AITKEN

AT BATU CAVES, KUALA LUMPUR

Cathedral or limestone factory of blunt stalagmites
in blast range of 2020 Visionaries
crunching bat guano under their boots. Graffiti.
Lost sandals. Landslip of a hundred-gross foldable chairs.
A cleaner's abandoned bucket.
A ladder climbs towards a forest skylight:
messages from the love-lost scroll down through ferns.
Scratched ventricles in a stucco Hindu heart
modelled in corrosive rain.

I'm glad it's not Jenolan.
Today's cave is moist with neon and dripping calcium.
Gifted with calm echoes, gods thrive
even on a working day — the worker's god that is.
The Brits then the Japs stockpiled bombs
where the gargoyle simians now fight
for hierarchy.
The Don with double-barrel fangs
slurps a 7-Up, squatting on a turquoise pergola.
Canines invest in peanut-filled handbags,
entrepreneurs mine human largesse.
On this day's mindblasting heat
dogs in shrink-wrapped ribs asking for nothing
like miscast Buddhists.

A souvenir bullwhip sir, and a BMW might absolve sin
but for you sir a mandala of skewers
one through each cheek and the tongue.
Virtue is not bleeding or wilting from the pain.
I too was excavated
by a different faith, nearly knifed to death
in Chinatown, my eyes were fake sapphires spit-polished in
          the dust.
The miraculous black peacock with tiger's head
guards the mystic portal
to my open-cut heart. Her eagle wings
folded for repose and authority.
From there two hundred steps
back to a carpet of pigeons
past the god of commerce dozing on an off day.
Baby-faced Ganesh, and the Winged Female Goat
swings her multiple udder, cosmic signage.

She'd be Going Places right now, my god,
though she'd never need to hurry, just browsing thanks
through a Bombay test pattern,
totalled by belief in a shop where Sue buys postcards
of Malaysian beaches
and Trengganu coconuts, and considers
a statuette of Kali
that might make sense
perched on the frost-free, guardian
of gourmet takeaways
two thousand miles away.

U-turn and we brood in traffic
detour through modern consciousness.
Not to include chaos must have been
a planning error.
For this view of modern curves and vistas
won't hide our scoured treeless hierarchies.
Everything's open too and precisely engineered
concrete city extracting its fee.
We don't ask to be meaningless, just driving home
or going to work, even
the hire car has its patron saint.
Make no mistake my friend:
the real temple, sir, is a god in love,
and a few to choose.

Meanjin

ERIC BEACH

WIMMERA EASTER SUNDAY

my brother hal's been jumping off th sydney harbour
bridge every easter sunday for twenty-eight years
& I'm getting sick of it
it's a long way to run from newtown & it's a hot day
& why did he stop halfway & chuck his trousers?
now my right eye's got this twitch
sometimes I feel like my son shane inherited hal's
suicide

they got on famously
it's been a great blue day
but one of those
nostril-pinching punch-drunk boxer days
my friends rescued me from
when I want to drown hal in th bath
for punching neville in his guts
so dad walked in took one look
& knocked me out
when dad knocked me out
I wouldn't say goodnight to him
no matter what!
he said I was like this
when I was three!

so I reckon that's when he lost
even before I took up chess
hal took up boxing
bagpipes
& th cops

had an nz police force epaullette
as bob dylan's motorbike mudguard
I had long orange hair down to my split-ends
& hung round with tattoos
when hal jumped dad said that they thought
it would have been me
I was disgusted
as though I knew what he meant

Salt-lick New Poetry

JUDITH BEVERIDGE

APPALOOSA

I have always loved the word guitar — DAVID ST. JOHN

I have never been bumped in a saddle as a horse springs
   from one diagonal to another,
         a two-beat gait, light and balanced,
as the four-beats per stride become the hair-blowing,
  wind-in-the-face, grass-rippling,
        muscle-loosening, forward-leaning
       exhilaration of the gallop.

And I have never counted the slow four-beat pace
  of distinct, successive hoofbeats
    in such an order as to be called *The Walk*.
Or learned *capriole*, *piaffe*, *croupade* in a riding school,
  nor heard the lingo of outback cattle-cutters
  spat out with their whip-ends and phlegm.

I have never stepped my hands over the flanks
  of a spotted mare; nor ridden a Cleveland Bay
carriage horse, or a Yorkshire coach horse;
  a French Percheron with its musical snicker;
    or a little Connemara its face buried
  in broomcorn, or in a bin of Wexford apples.

I have never called a horse Dancer, Seabiscuit, Ned,
   Nellie, Trigger or Chester, or made clicking
  noises with my tongue, the fifty kilometres
     to town with a baulking gelding and a green
quartertop buggy. Nor stood in a field while
  an old nag worked every acre,
  only stopping to release difficult knobs of manure,
and swat flies with her tail. And though I have

waited for jockeys at the backs of stables
in the mist and rain, for the soft feel of their riding silks
and saddles, for the cool smoke of their growth-stunting
   cigarettes, for the names of the yearlings
     and mares they whisper along with the names
of horse-owning millionaires — ah, more, more even
than them — I have always loved the word *appaloosa*.

Salt-lick New Poetry

ELIZABETH BLACKMORE

DOG BITE

my dog did this I grab my arm to keep it shut no blood
but from the holes ooze yellow worms of fat you got rid
of the dog of course a question from the stern intern as he
patches and sews the greyness of shock spares me from
    answering

After the stitching my arm sprouted black whiskers.

Blue Dog: Australian Poetry

JANICE BOSTOK

THE WIDOW

the second-hand skivvy chokes as
efficiently as a stranger in an alleyway
who doesn't know his victim but vents
his hate just the same blue veins
protruding like the eyes of a cosmetic
queen home from her third face lift she
tries to place two fingers between the
collar and neck for the same protection
afforded by anyone to a pet dog a
consideration which she would never
allow her husband when he was alive

Salt-lick New Poetry

PETER BOYLE AND MTC CRONIN

OBJECTS OF YOU IN WATER

SPOON

The river has changed its name
though the two banks sit eyeing each other,
the row of blank totem stones
reflected back and forth
in the vanishing that joins them.
Incident number one: a drawing of a spoon
floated by before snagging on an overhanging root
of willow exposed by the land's
deathward leap. Always
your face in the sky
etched by itinerant leaves
and that wistful passion of just seeing you
in the ordinary blaze of things —
one more step along a journey home.

CHANDELIER DROP

We don't talk of crystal balls anymore
but in one is where I imagined you.
Why are words so cute you hang them in your room for
    hours?

Why are flies more austere than monoliths?
Why do you enter my mouth like a wasp
to set fake aphorisms buzzing?

Who twisted us around so we can never move in the one story,
our histories all wrong, and set us both down
maimed and beautiful
exactly right?

SAUCEPAN

Sometimes I see you held inside a cradlesong
but then you are already cradling a saucepan
or setting off across muddy streets,
your hiking boots filled with purpose …

Or is it you, at the door, with a new smile,
your hands filled with coriander root,
a recipe?

You left your old life aboard a boat
on a river of domesticity —
what an odd thing to break my heart,
such erotic bravery.

BOWL AND ICE

Later, from distraction, your thumb
with its small cushion of flesh untipped
by the serrated knife immersed

in a bowl of ice and you laugh drinking wine
above the sea turning to blood
as I continue to cut.

In the tree beyond the kitchen window,
the shadow of its small inhabitant
soundless and drawing us
into the dark.

BRIDGE

It's a technical term, though no less poetic for that,
not these words, but the one not here,
the bird that flew from the post
in the direction of its older suitor, the earth.
Incident two or three is forgotten.
Number four has to do with you looking away,
towards what I thought was a bird on a railway bridge
but I watched all day and it didn't fly.
You shook compassion into the sky from a cloth you held
between your freezing fingers.
For you, the small figure of the eagle
disappeared through the metal arch
as the train passed beneath it,
solid and holy before the seven-branched tracks.
Which way will we go today?

PORTABLE ROADWAY

All that the sea can mean —
the place we are going to.
What use there is fire?
The sunlight was all inside us,
all our food gone on offerings
the gods never eat.

The sky was closed down
so you brought the road with you —
the one line from your mouth to the horizon

                                        coming apart —
distance stinging your tongue with words unrecallable as
        days,
tomorrow and yesterday opening their lips to the tithe,
imitating your littoral cry.

WATER-JUG

I sat on the verandah where the sky was drifting in,
the lines of small white flocks — the dead coming back
the way they had always threatened to.
The large water-jug, at least one hundred years old,
becomes part of my hand — raised over the roof
where the poor live — passionless,
intent on my own mouth.
Momentarily
I am the watcher in a lighthouse.
There is the ship, surrounded by the birds of the dead.
It is full of reports. Of cups for this falling water.

CEILING FOR BALCONY

Incident number six:
pulled the balcony ceiling down and forced all the juveniles to
    fly or fall.
Today the sky is in my blood.
Were you already married to that galaxy when we met?
You moved so fast I couldn't tell.

LIPS

I was frightened when I first saw you changing, your face
unravelling into pain that was also anger and also
all emotion shutting down.
Like the pigeons you murdered,
bits of other lives fluttered screaming
stuck onto your face.
It was like making love but in reverse —
your eyes dilated with otherness,
your lips that didn't move:
'You know, none of us are here.'

LADLE

Coffee and curry steam in the same kitchen,
their hindu-hispanic fragrance
staining the dull air —
a night garden where the trees
split themselves open.
It's always serious,

the town you grew up in.
Those who are taken away.
Those who stay as if the present was a longer place
than anywhere else.

Myself — the self that relinquishes all at night
to the night — I never left this city,
slightly travelling nowhere — to the world
and then on great wings to the brief land of autobiography.
It has as little room to roam in as love.
Everyone there is pressed unbearably
against themselves
and when they try to build other-ships
the world sinks from the weight
of their tools.
It was when I bent to retrieve my hammer
that I first saw your face, your hand
with a ladle
of different glass.

UNNAMED OBJECT

The ninth incident came after several undiscussable
because our lovemaking we kept
quite private.
It was short and sharp.
You said,
I am never going to feel your pain.

SEA BIRD EATEN BY ANTS

Who knows when these scattered feathers
adjourned from the sky.

The carcass of a white sea bird
offers sand that will be hard-won
to the loose waves of low-tide.

An ant, I remember, tickles the flesh
of your hand.

Between its jaws a whole other world
crashes through
the lit universe.

NEEDLE

I unstitch words from your arm.
Your eyes smoulder with fire and hurt.
The leaves have coloured your eyes
with the day I was trying to find.
The wind in my garden
and the soft start of rain
make me think of you.
If you come back into the world
I will let go of my pain.

UMBILICAL CORD

The least of you goes on
holding tight to the world,
circling like the long arm of a monster trapped in the pool —
longing has no part in these assessments.
Three years since our breaking
the ice preserves a strange nudity of lost flesh,
some sharp butchered instinct that walks away
and still carries
the listless name of earth.

MARKER BUOYS

Simply a pen scratching on a page
or rats feeding in a disused warehouse —
my journey to you
from this long night of the illuminated kitchen
drifting out to sea in the darkness of space.
When I lost that sense of you speaking from inside me
I felt I had swum a first mile
out into the strong black current
that cuts below each shoreline.

URN

Where is the thirteenth ocean?
This unlucky number is mine.
I count it with memories, dumbness, your hands
that I see in every one of life's images:

a boy rubbing his head into the back of a man's neck;
so many different jasmines, wildful,
pretending delicacy for the swallows, the ashes.
The urn falls through the floor at midday:
Whom you all love is fortune,

                         is love.

DRIFTING, ASSORTED

The marina moored against the grey ache of summer,
this slow lapping
where all the sky banks up.
Objects of you in water:
the ankle or the eye
the shoelace the boating pole the cup and saucer
and the soap rinsed off your hands
in a sink of darkness
where the moon sifts the rice:
all held in a transparent world
where I could name you
and bless
our vanishing.

SKETCHING PAD

The river wound its way back from the future
to its own mouth.
Still the stones lay, still they erected themselves
                         in silence.

You drew me in the forest once.

My face in the leaves as if it could fall away from everything
just as easily.

In the scratched lines of your pencil

I was to be the wound opened in remembrance.

All incidents shed in words.

Southerly

Elizabeth Campbell

LETTERS TO THE TREMULOUS HAND

i.

it is usual
several scribes in this case *A*, *B* and
The Tremulous Hand
who among their duties
copied many bibles psalms illustrated
or not as in the case of these
twenty manuscripts

a long career
stretching perhaps into
absence of name or grave we may speculate
five catalogued states of the hand's
probably genetic infirmity five layers
of glossing categorized
chronologically mainly marginal some interlinear
earliest-known Middle English Nicene Creed

fifty thousand
Old English (by then defunct
referred to hereon as OE) lemmata glossed (see
appended index of most common
mostly in Latin sometimes his contemporary

Middle English (now
defunct and abbreviated in this test as ME)
a plain hand
devoid of embellishment (see plate

a Herbal
the scribe preoccupied with bladder stones
sore eyes this one full text well-known *Soul's Address
to the Body* derived of course
from *Song of Solomon* (which should be thought
the origin of this sort of vernacular poem
all poor reflections of their source
and this a fragment

spelling corrected
marginal notes few lines of music
one quotation on what it means
to pray to Jesus though that comment not recorded here
in light brown ink mostly
but not exclusively religious by the end
decided learning to the left the
wobble most pronounced
in the vertical stroke
toward the body

ii.

Dear Hand
beloved Tremulosius brother
teach me a difference

between divine truth and cramping.
Suspicious of anything
that could be called expansive —

edges impinging
as if seen through tears — I know the soul
is only ever its soul

in the most precise place — tongue
quivering unto the wrist breath
a thin skin tearing

like pinned order — I am
suspicious of anything reductive — sex
is strange but many things

are stranger than sex — bees
have nested in my lion.
But all this clearly flattens

like the blotting-out of sin — like the Earth
I am on not in
O urge to fleetness! tedious epiphany
wings flight wings
ugiquitous as clothes

LIDIJA CVETKOVIC

A SEED, A CRUTCH, A HEART

from the pig's slit throat a red carpet unrolls
all his life he's been fed for this

the matron of honour lays birds' eggs in her braid
they'll seal the nuptial kiss with their hatching

the bride's kin descend from the hills making wide gestures
with splintered hands, carrying the scent of humus and wolves

they meet at crossroads and laugh through the ruins of their teeth
as they hand the groom a gun

when he shoots the apple off the bride's head
a seed flies into her eye and grows into a seedling

clumsy virgins flirt with guests' lapels, pin rosemary
for fidelity, flaunt drops of blood from pricked fingers

the bride holds back from pulling a loose thread
off the priest's vestment lest it unstitch him

she back-flips her bouquet towards a young widow
marked with mourning, but the wind blows it back

the groom's hand mounts the bride's over the knife
his thumb crushes a frosted rose beneath the arbour

when midnight snips the marionette strings
the bride and groom collapse, cannot hold each other up

            *   *   *

the groom chops the slender apple tree
and carves crutches, etches a heart on her iris

_____

Heat

LUKE DAVIES

---

from TOTEM POEM

In the yellow time of pollen, in the blue time of lilacs,
in the green that would balance on the wide green world,
air filled with flux, world-in-a-belly
in the blue lilac weather, she had written a letter:
You came into my life really fast and I liked it.

When we let go the basket of the good-luck birds
the sky erupted open in the hail of its libation;
there was a gap and we entered it gladly. Indeed the birds
may have broken the sky and we, soaked, squelched
in the mud of our joy, braided with wet-thighed surrender.

In the yellow time of pollen near the blue time of lilacs
there was a gap in things. And here we are.
The sparrows flew away so fast a camera could not catch them.
The monkey swung between our arms and said *I am, hooray,*
the monkey of all events, the great gibbon of convergences.

We were falling towards each other already &
the utter abandon to orbits was delicious.
The falcon rested on the little man's arm and falconry
was the High Path of the World. Whole minutes passed.
We were falling and the jungle fell with us.

She said *I came, I came to my senses really fast*
and you liked it. I was surrounded by the fluttering
of wings, nothing but a whirring in my ears,
and the whole earth tilted and I lost my reason.
For a time falconry was the high path of the world.

At night the sky was filled with animals.
Ganesh loomed large among those points of light.
He said *Change!* and we said *Lord we are ready*
to bend. Thou art the high exalted most flexible.
He said *Then I will enter into your very dreams.*

And the yellow-tailed black cockatoo, ablaze
in his own musculature, soared all night above the sunlit
fields of whisky grass that stretched inside me
to a river's edge. The great bird cawed its majesty,
a sonic boom; and even I was barely welcome there.

There was a gap in things; and all the lilacs bloomed.
Words split in our grasp. We were licking the cream
from the universal ice. Words foundered and cracked.
How the bonnet was warm on your bottom! And the metal
continued tick-ticking though the engine was off.

And the evening shuddered, since everything is connected.
I was licking the cream from the universal saucer.
I was all of Cheshire and points between.
You saw the great sky turn blacker, you saw the spray of stars
& your hair got tangled in the windscreen wiper.

At the hot ponds we stripped as night closed in.
I secretly admired your underwear, your long
elusive legs. In the spring where we lay side by side
we held hands. Up above the steam the sky. I said
that one is called Sirius or Dog Star, but only here on Earth.

And when since the stories foretold it we parted,
those birds were all released again. Such buoyancy.
They go on forever like that. How else to say thankyou
in a foreign place? We are ever in the arms of our exile,
forever going one way and the other

though sometimes of course on a sphere that is not so bad.
I will meet you on the nape of your neck one day,
on the surface of intention, word becoming act.
We will breathe into each other the high mountain tales,
where the snows come from, where the waters begin.

In the yellow time of pollen when the fields were ablaze
we were very near bewildered by beauty.
The sky was a god-bee that hummed. All the air boomed
with that thunder. It was both for the prick
and the nectar we drank that we gave ourselves over.

And if every step taken is a step well-lived but a foot
towards death, every pilgrimage a circle, every flight-path
the tracing of a sphere: I will give myself over and over.
I have migrated through Carpathians of sorrow
to myself heaped happy in the corner there.

Nothing seemed strange in the world, you'll understand —
nothing ever more would. Monkey Boy came to me saying
Look — the moon of the moon. The little one circled the big one.
He crouched in the palm of my hand, tiny, sincere,
pointing at the sky. There was something sad about him.

The python was nothing, nothing at all, nothing
but strength shed to suppleness, nothing but will
encased in itself. The python was a muscle of thought.
Coiled and mute, in a place where nothing but rain fell,
the python thought: this is the beginning or end of the world.

The python was everywhere, everywhere at once, aware
only too much of that ageless agony: its existence.
I am tired, it said; and the stream burbled by.
I am waiting for the recoil, the uncoil, coil of night,
coil of stars, coil of the coldness of the water.

The python said: who are these people?
The whole city sweated, moved like a limb. The air
fitted like a glove two sizes too small and too many
singers sang the banal. The bars roared all night.
The kite-hawks grew ashamed. All nature squirmed.

In the yellow time of pollen there's a certain slant of light
that devours the afternoon, and you would wait forever
at the Gare de l'Est, if time stood still, if she would come.
She is the leopard then, its silvery speed; where will you
wrestle her, and in what shadows, and on what crumpled sheets?

And all those sheets were pampas and savannas, the soft expanses
of all that would be absent forever, all that was
past, and future, and not here. And in a white rose
there were not to be found any secrets, since in its unfolding
there was no centre, nor in its decay. Only the random petals fallen.

In the yellow time of poppies when the fields were ablaze
those invisible pollens rained around us.
The days held us lightlocked in golden surrender
& all night long the night shot stars.
When my chest unconstricted at last, did yours?

The real issue, of course, was this: atomically, energetically,
everything was wave function. And a wave continues forever into space,
the wavelength never alters, only the intensity lessens, so
in the worst cosmic way everything is connected by vibrations.
And this, as even a dog would know, is no consolation.

Ah but the dogs will save us all in the end & even the planet.
Not the superdogs but the household friendlies, always
eager to please, hysterically fond, incessant, carrying in the very
wagging of their tales an unbounded love not even
therapists could imagine; their forgiveness unhinges us.

We were reduced to this: this day and night,
primary gold and indigo, the binary profusion
of distances guessed at, heat and cold, colours
logged in the retina and lodged in the spine;
we were dogs who knew the infinite is now,

that celandine was buttercup, that buttercup was marigold.
The dog-star marked the dog days & the wild rose
was dog rose. The crow's-foot was wild hyacinth.
By day the correspondences were clear.
I walked across the whin land. Speedwell bluer than sky.

A practised ear could hear, between two breaths,
deep space wherein the mind collects itself.
Words foundered and cracked. *Nearly*
never bulled the cow. A shining isomorphousness
rang out. The roussignol sang all night.

All colours were shuffled endlessly but never lost.
A practised ear could hear, between two breaths,
the secret blackness of the snow
come flooding in. On summer's lawns
the ice-melt sprayed its figure-eights from sprinklers.

And everything stopped working, second time around,
as if it had never happened before. Fans
moved the corpses of fireflies through the rooms,
supplicant, pathetic, pleading in brittle postures.
Everything was magnified by their bug-eyed deaths.

We became solemn in that profusion
of dying. Cane toads fattened the asphalt
in the mist and the rain; our headlights caught them
tensed as if listening: they were waiting,
mute, for the imbecility of eternity.

The clocks merely pulsed, or rather the days.
Like shotgun spray on the weatherboard, sleep
scattered itself through the blurred heat
and secreted itself in the nooks of delirium.
Sometimes the magpies would wake us, or the phone,

mid-afternoon. And we needed nothing, not even hope,
being no different from the dragonflies,
or the cows in their despair. It appeared we lived
on sunlight and chocolate bars. You blossomed
so from not ever reading the newspapers.

Things came and went — the years and all the airports.
I was a shade scattering my shade seed
liberally to the winds and weather-vanes.
There was not enough absence to go round.
I heard voices, *stabat mater*, in the whine of jets

and in air vents and headphones a stream
trilling over rocks. On tarmacs and in transit
I saw your lips, your nakedness, the trees,
that dappled light. I dreamt of orchards.
The preciseness of the world came flooding in.

For every blossom there could be no turning back,
one path only to cup and fig, beyond
the belly of the heart's content, each precipice
a flood of salt and jewels. Tang
of the overwhelming, flooding in.

I saw a kestrel quiver but not move
high in the air as if a sculptor left it
unattended, incomplete, just waiting for
a sign, just give me an excuse. I heard
the bush rat squeal. For there is nothing

lost may not be found if sought.
The minotaur in the corral
who called himself Asterion
tramples me softly with his song &, frustrated,
head-butts the posts. I can but admire him.

In the yellow time of pollen when the air was weighed down
there were bees plump with syrup. There were figs
fit to burst at the seams. I understood
how language had emerged: in the Flesh of the Fruit.
I spoke my tongues against your breathlessness.

Down there nothing but eternity and praise.
To be alive I had to praise, to praise I had to
learn to speak. Speak loudly though to drown
the blood about to burst, to drown eternity
whose howl floods every canyon into nothingness.

In the blue time of lilacs the last colour standing
was the mauve that jacarandas leak when all else
has gone grey: last glow before night,
the brightest that earth ever gave. Far across
the estuary the mangroves rippled in the rain.

Pelicans plumped on the tide-posts, world-in-a-belly.
There was mud for the taking. The orb spiders
clung during storms to the high-tensile webs.
Much later the fruit bats, insane with greed, tore into the fig trees
and gnashed at the edges of dreams.

Time was merely the measure of motion
with respect to before and after. Meanwhile
the universe expands. The pine trees creaked.
The pine cones cracked. On a windless day there was time
to dream of you. The pine cones snapped open the silence.

All the fields and force fields stretched away to snow caps.
Gravitational, magnetic — there were even fields undreamt of;
and the green one where we lay, where we organised to meet,
where the wildflowers parted and the gorse looked like light,
was hidden in the cleft our kisses made.

Light stretches as it moves away. The peaks and contours
we explored had taught us time was malleable. All things
have mass except ideas. A hammock was therefore a metaphor like
breathe. A diamond meant nothing but *carbon-later-on*.
The flight paths of the pelicans smelled … like *luck*.

We were falling and the jungle fell with us.
It rained all through the pass; at every plateau praise.
World-in-a-belly. From the photon's point of view
the universe contracted to one point
and even as it left it had arrived.

To us the photon spread through space
in studious propagation. In an ocean the waves
had water to ride on, and sound waves fought their way
through air. But light was the medium itself.
Thousands of birds, the tiniest birds, adorned your hair.

In the driest season I drew my love from geometry.
I cried to learn a circle was a curve
of perfect equidistance from a point. In summer
wild sage grew in tufts on the slopes
where in spring the sun would melt the snows to scree.

All the while I was asking myself what was the
howling outside the hut I was mistaken I couldn't
recognise my own voice it was so loud I was having
trouble with inside and outside. You came to me
from God knows where in wider arcs than birds can make.

You made me calm. I said to God *God*
how often do I thank you God? I had had
so many years of beauty intruding on all I did I did
not think it might intrude on others. Others
showed no signs of it. But you said laughing *Taste it Taste it*.

And a wet front smothered the whole south coast &
our hazard lights flashed in the cloud of unknowing &
the semis overtook us and blinded us with spray.
I said to God *God I am speechless I am*
contented I am very tired and I am rather in love.

Heat

B RUCE D AWE

FOR ANNIE

(and for Liz whose family history research brought you to life)

To find I had a sister
(twenty-seven years before
I made it to this sinister
bright world) fills me with awe ...

You died in your first year
but learning of you still
bemuses: where there were four
of us, now the incalculable

abacus of time has added
another bead to the row
(young losses are most dreaded,
each comes as a brute blow

to expectation, like those times
you prop and someone then
bumps into you, or those games
of musical chairs that betoken

a player caught between
one chair and the next)
— Annie. I didn't mean
these reflections as a text

on unpreparedness
(one will be taken, and one left)
but rather sought to express
my belated thanks for the gift

of knowledge which I owe
to no-one here but Liz
— a belated sad Hello
is all this poem is ...

Southerly

JAN DEAN

SIGNED AUGUSTE RODIN

Chérie, your letter implied I was obsessed
with stone. Granted, as a boy I scanned the pile

for flat ones of just the right weight to skim across
the river, rubbed them in my palms, delighted

in their feel, rejoiced when I found the unblemished.
Stones with special attributes like the marks of a zebra

I stored in lieu of marbles saved by friends.
When I skimmed them I was thrilled by

the flick of the wrist. The movement of actors
literary figures and politicians was sublime.

All inhabited characters other than their own.
The man I became was present in the child.

Subtraction was fine but I liked addition more. Nothing
could compare to the squelch of clay and the way

the sun blessed it with fissures, as if to say
you've done well, my son. My figures were energised

from within. They caught the light but were made
by shadows, imbuing drama and mystery.

Modelling in clay or wax was my forte.
When molten bronze replaced the wax that seeped

away, my work could be multiplied for the enjoyment
of the bourgeoisie. A humble heart should never

suppress a generous spirit. Your tableau charmed
but I wouldn't want to leave the wrong impression.

Blue Dog: Australian Poetry

TIM DENOON

CLOVELLY

The blue groper bloats its gills
and hardly notices the two of us
snorkelling like corpses on the cold surface.
His hand draws away like a split oyster
yellow Speedos flaring like a mango skin.
My mask fogs up when I try to speak
where did you meet him
or where did you love him
but all I can see are two legs
tapering out like water kites
as his flippers flex gently with the current.

Island

DAN DISNEY

ECCE HOMBRE

A thing eats a thing
and is then ate
by another thing. This thing
not lasting long, is ate
by a further thing;
the further thing ate by something again
ate soon after by something else. This thing
is trapped and ate by another thing
which is then ate
by a thing. And so
it goes. This thing
kidnapped and fattened with small things
by a biggish thing
is ate.
The biggish thing-fattening thing
(ambushed, carried 'twixt a pole
to a rocky place with no garden)
is put in a stewing pot and ate
by a thing, which is ate
by some other thing
ate soon after
by something else. This thing is ate by another thing
called Craig. And thus it goes!

Craig, though never perhaps believing in the unstoppable
    nature of
destiny
is also ate. The eater of Craig
has no name. A thing, conjoined from the outset
eats the thing with no name that ate Craig
and is tackled sometime later
by two other things joined only
by hunger
who pick at bones in the dark below the moon dogs howl at.
Later, a town of things eats a town of other things.
Right down to the huts and family portraits.
A colony of bedraggled and limping stray things
eats them as they return home but you'd expect that sort of
    behaviour
from things like those.
And thus it goes!
A thing with a paunch and silver monocle
conducts a cogged factory
where things package up other things for resale in polystyrene
with bbq sauce.
Fat kahuna things loll and burp in the gentle night
in their lockdown rooms in the sky
above the canker of gutter things
being ate
by gutter things.
Dawn things eat night things chewing dusk things on day
    things

swallowed by the footstepping time thing
devoured in turn by the thing-that-has-no-words thing.
And thus it goes! Wind things
eat windless things,
thing things bite and gnaw at nothing things,
mad screaming things suck the marrow of whisper things.
The star things eat bits of the heavens thing.
A thing, eating a thing, gets ate by another thing
but
somewhere a horse made of bullion has begun to sink to the
      bottom
of a soundless sea
and is declared a permanent mystery
(not to mention inedible).
And so it goes.

Journal of Australian Studies:
Creative Arts Review

LAURIE DUGGAN

BRITISH COLUMBIA FIELD NOTES

1

Japanese brides drink red wine in the rose garden;
patches of snow (all the way from here to Hokkaido).

2

The inhabitants of this continent eat potatoes for breakfast
their coffee is German (or Polish) not Italian;
they mix the sweet with the savoury.

The house could be in Wolverhampton
the apartments, Irkutsk;
from Beacon Hill the horizon is American.

Seabirds (sooty gulls? Pacific gulls?)
appear outsize on the entablatures.
Techno resonates from a distant car.

Attached to the old meridian,
a siren carries me back to Brisbane.
When I wake I don't know where I am.

3

From an old photograph, the movement of redwoods,
heads and faces imposed upon stages of totem;
deities vomited up outside the weatherboards.

4

Circa 1890
jail sentences imposed for potlatch because
the government thought it was wrong
that the people should receive, gratis, sewing machines;

an assumption that existence, no longer considered
'primitive'
                    should obey
the laws of economics
(all other kinds of transaction,
politics, art
                    subsumed or erased
as extravagant or
unnecessary entities.

Item: a silver mask
partly burnt
                    on entry
into the Christian life.

Smallpox 1862,
again, in Vancouver, 1888-90.

In the period of measured history
the events are too familiar:
logging, the fur trade, mineral extraction;

on the flat calm of Georgia Strait
chained timbers float,
the beach shored up with dead wood.

Advent   1843 or thereabouts.

5

In the hall beneath the smoke hole
shadows give life to shapes
discovered in redwood trunks
(beaks and other protuberances added on),

figures produced from figures,
from the womb or from the mouth,
as naming regenerates the dead
(and the sur-name, imposed,

breaks this continuity for another:
the purpose of statistics and control,
a hunt for 'the family'
as normative ethnology.

6

The Provincial Legislature appears
'like the Brighton Pavilion
backed by the Himalayas': a Brighton
gargantuan and colourless;

                      high Victoriana
larger than the governance halls of whole nations.

The Empress Hotel — 1908
built on reclaimed land

(back at this smaller establishment
a light well, grimy astroturf at its base,
rear of a nearby hotel
its regular windows,
a low sky over placed water of James Bay

(invisible from here).

7

Though the air chills
the thick green is summer,
a late light on the horizon,
across the esplanade
moored bulk carriers
the wooded park at UBC.

Cirrus clouds grid
at cross-purpose, around the point
in the wind of English Bay,

the colours of buildings luminous
against the clouds, the shadowed mountains;

two yellow cones of sulphur
across Burrard Inlet, a space
beneath the bridge (the Lion Gate)
denoted *Indian Reserve* #5.

8

Emily Carr's cowled or hooded trees,
her grids of darkness and light

(the provincial dilemma: is the work overvalued
regionally? nationally? because she's 'ours'?)

those vertical totems, the trees themselves
and what shadows they make available;

under the cool white dome of the Vancouver gallery
these charcoals imitate the sky, cirrus and crossbar,

as I catch the trolley back to West End.

9

Apartments date mainly from the 1950s,
an erasure of wooden housing from the city to Stanley Park.

Burrard Inlet is still a working harbour
(containers, sulphur and woodchips)

logs chained, floating downstream
the odd escapee beached and weathered

fit for sunbathers to shelter, leeward from ocean wind
or rest a bicycle against.

10

The disposition of things.

Neighbourhoods of a strange city
escape from the map;
a district without _____ [name the missing
      convenience].

These tall glass buildings
in front of snow patches,

mountains at the end of every street.

11

Hotel ceilings creak,
beams visible through plaster,

voices audible;
an extractor groans.

From the bus stop you can look down, either direction
to Burrard Inlet or English Bay.

12

Go to where the trees cross the numbers
to spend money near Arbutus and 4th,

Kitsilano; the houses protected
by security firms, back onto the water

as the city towers appear, whitened
in a bleaching wind, against the mountains and clouds;

to Green College, UBC — Arts & Crafts in an English
          garden,
bagels over the Georgia Strait

(below, on Third Beach: rocks
woodchips, nudists and Italian fishermen.

13

Bill Reid's
glacial curvature of bird shapes
fits the materials
to the landscape
and the body
(fine delineations
of a bracelet).

Old people tell each other what's happening
as they read museum labels, dramatising the educative;

a Haida man
spends all day in a dark room
explaining.

14

Victoria below, then, south, the Olympics,
Washington State's snow ridges.

Cartoon birds on a washed-out screen.

Diagonally back, two Canadian business men
(retired) register anecdotes and statistics

all the way to Honolulu.

Heat

CHRIS EDWARDS

THE AWFUL TRUTH

Despite the vast data at hand
pertaining to his belief
in the charm and ease of exposure,
not much is known about Cary
beyond the simple decency
and consular good manners
his roles only occasionally
allowed him to exhibit.
The outbreak of war
had offered him boy scouts
on the docks, followed by a few
last letters to post, about which he was
curious but remained none the wiser.
Still, a pattern began to emerge
as if from the wallpaper
of his bedroom — a patter
too, like roaches. Formidable
omens? Probably not. Probably
just roaches.

Australian Book Review

LIAM FERNEY

ANGEL

it happens in a crucible in a small
motel on the edge of a highway tucked
between a fast food joint and a factory
every afternoon we religiously skim
the tabloids and the newspapers glazed
sunglasses blocking out the glare and fizzy
drinks sipped from deckchairs a pot plant
totters on the brink of falling the wind gusts
it smashes on the ochre tiles mexican-
orange shards share the canvas with black
dirt that we'll neglect to sweep up for months
the whole time dog day afternoon loops in the
living room pacino with a gun his shirt soggy
with sweat and an antique clock ticks like an
aerosol can shaken on a train platform

we stayed up all night taking drugs till it hurt
to smile and the airplanes bank low over the
smog and reveal to us something telling yet
silent and the future is a trajectory of fantasy
as we spend our tired lives wrapped in the
spoils of outrageous fortune the ancient carpets
a vase plundered from greece and a stolen

klimt hangs in the living room and you stare
at a rainbow reflected from a crystal as the
sun begins to set all this happens in a city
we don't remember and to prove it we sell up
and move to the ocean and I remember something
bukowski once said the way to end a poem like
this is to become suddenly quiet you do that and
the television explodes into the white desert night

_____

Southerly

KRIS HEMENSLEY

THE HAPPINESS OF WINTER

Now the train sits at Collingwood where the High Rise
exudes brooding & pain. I gaze at the dark clouds

beneath the city's blue rim and see they're carrying
night and not a dirty day's rain. Walking home

with this vision from Clifton Hill to the Creek
should've blessed him I think remembering the dill

sat opposite me smoking his bitter fag to the butt.
Silently cursed him instead. Bagged his disregard.

Looking up at the sky I reckon it's clearer now than
moments before. The day frames the Creek like a mirror

and glowering in the middle is that desolate boy's face.
Unreachable and unreadable. Wretched it is that a hoy

couldn't fetch him to another place. An hello to initiate
a kind of conversion as surely was once the case?

Bus's upper-deck & train a smoky buzz back then.
Workers' & students' end of day. Luck in the air. One or a
    dozen

up to you. Of anyone & everything to pursue. Suddenly
there are kids top of Urquhart Street varying footy rules

as kids without a sou'll always do. Here to the light-pole
then to the centre of the road they'll duel for a point.

A kick on the full at their strange papa's roller-door
earns six more. That's how it is. And so I'm propelled

to the happiness of Winter.

Salt-lick New Poetry

Rae Desmond Jones

EL NIÑO

after one day when the spring rain whispered down through
    the dry air,
washing the soft topsoil from the hard clay underneath
& drumming the corrugated iron of the garage
i go out into the yard.

    during the depression families planted carrots & potatoes
        in the shadow
    between the tumbledown shed & the fence where now
    the tendrils of a mulberry tree strangle the scrubby
        grapefruit
    hunched in the corner to keep out the world.
the mulberry is larger & stronger
& must triumph yet the grapefruit defies my knowledge of
    darwin
& my ignorance of courage by producing a crop
of clustered fruit now rotting on the ground.

fallen fruit is tainted. my mother intended a metaphor
but she grew up on a farm as strong as any man:
for seven years before she died her empty body sprinted the
    corridors
of a sterile nursing home, pursued by a nurse

with a tray of pills.
>when I asked what I could do
>the sister responded in broad scots that
>fruit would be valuable because *their* food
>was manufactured in bulk.

when i returned a week later the undead were watching
>television
in dressing gowns but my mother had entrenched herself in a
>corner
behind a wardrobe & flayed the air with a rolled up copy of
>the women's weekly.
>>She paused & her clear dark eyes locked on me when i
>>>offered
>>a bag of bananas & apples & a bunch of cherries.

it doesn't matter you know sister drawled *she isn't there any
>longer*
but mother's hard muscled impertinence & her stare of
>unflinching disdain
showed that she was there.

>i drag the green Otto bin
>from the shed although its small plastic wheels sink into
>>the dirt.
>it has been years since i ate grapefruit.
slowly & methodically I lift each pulpy sod & lob it into the
>bin

then pluck the last lobe on the tree
& take it inside the house to cut it open.
   despite its tough skin it tastes clean
   & effervescent grief explodes in the back of my throat

_____

Meanjin

Aileen Kelly

MOOD / TENSE

She's camped well out in the subjunctives.
Were she to stay in this thin scenario
(jerrybuilt frames, splash of distemper,
in a slight breeze the uneasy paperbarks
rustling, lamenting *Had one but thought …*)
despite conditional character make-up
and a camouflage mosquito net
lest anyone come — the last syntax purist? —

imperatives would heavy her sleep:
Come home. Listen, act normal. Don't be a fool.

She juggles her billy and bed-roll.
Sighs. Treks towards some indicative suburb.
And perhaps she can settle between
concrete floors and walls, the oil-coloured people.
Within some future she will concede
though her tense balance has never been perfect
her civil heart beats: *present, present.*

Blue Dog: Australian Poetry

Emma Lew

SUGARED PATH

Thanks for coming by so late in such a beautiful
state of mind. The stars dream this way. We
can't keep running from the past. The stones
on the road: like I said, it's just a hunch. You
won't be smiling much longer because I'm starting
to remember things about my life.

Relax, it's not
what you're thinking. You saved my life, you
nursed me back to health. First day of spring.
Let's face it: you screwed up. I find myself trying
to believe in the void and it's got me a little
confused.

This is a city of terrible fire. That's
the problem. I've got you to hold onto. It's not
the life I would have chosen, so keep the air off
of me. History's still in rough shape, I guess that
answers my question.

Truth, love and happiness,
that's the direction I'm headed. Look at the facts:
I'm supposed to be a fountain of tears. We're
back where we started, the darkest part of
the whole garden, and that's the past sitting right
over there. There's a tidal wave coming, I just

always assumed.

It's a one in a million chance,
but it's possible. I'm talking about you lighting up
like a storm. I could have accepted your gift, but
I'm wiser, I've learned from my mistakes. I'd sign
anything for daylight again.

_____

Meanjin

KATHRYN LOMER

ON THE TONGUE

1 TONGUE-TIED

They have taken away my books, and I am naked;
I want to pull down the sky like a blue comforter.
When a nurse brings a warmed blanket
I cry for the gesture of a mother.
Next they will extract a piece of my tongue
from among secret filaments of wet flesh,
one which has tasted the salt-sour of your semen.
I'm reminded of this morning's tongue-and-groove,
the phallic aspiration of the muscle in our mouths
and the ways we try to clamber into another's body.
Perhaps now my tongue will be less sharp
when it comes to licking old wounds;
they say there will be no scar tissue.
A foul spray panics me: to swallow
seemed such a simple act this morning.
They inject some relaxation
and I sing the nurse a tongue-twister.
For three days I will be tongue-tied,
without puffs of air to hold me at word's length.
In some countries those who lie
have their tongues cut out. Imagine
the empty red cavity, the hollow scream

filling long days. Nylon lashings
scratch at my gums. Tongues
will wag, my mother used to say
to her teenage daughter, home late.
Her tongue now a fistful of dust,
mine unable to answer back.

2   GIFT OF TONGUES

Babies react to the mother tongue
heard in the womb, fists furious and the suck
of their own tongues frantic at syllables;
they babble — da da —
rejecting the language of belly and breast.
Children fill their heads with words
and ways to put them together;
watch their effect with wonder.
They spend their hoard but never go bust;
they are richer than kings, who seem to say little
and have others speak. Poor kings.
Tongues have always worked well on skin,
leaving wet trails like the snail
in places which seem to have waited
forever for this, and this. Tasting sweet
at the front, bitter at the back.
Yet the tongue's pleasures of taste and touch
have bowed to the chattering beast:
litanies lurch from our mouths —
hymns and endearments, lies and laments,

declarations of war.
Sometimes the tongue is used like a stock-race gate
to divide into pens and brand;
they don't speak the language, a foreign tongue
the accent always on difference;
not for nothing is it named blade.
If we understood this gift
we would drum on the palate again and again
the open alveolar L of love,
the dark L deep in the mouth, but still love;
we would kiss with our tongues.

3   A CUTTING TONGUE

For three days words have been dammed;
I've had utter freedom to drift in thought,
moving from defined and lined-up
to a pinpoint of being, a stillness
behind the eyes, silent as our beginnings in the womb
where the child unfurls like a fern frond,
when the tongue is but a pattern of proteins,
and the complex circuitry for hearing things
has yet to be installed. In the waiting room
a man asks for the time but I ignore him,
intrigued by a boy and girl conversing in sign.
I envy the way they carve three cubic feet of air
into slices of meaning,
fingers for vocab, faces for grammar,
free of the fight between larynx and lung

so that underwater they might talk
as casually as you and I over coffee.
I would like to write my poems this way,
handfuls of meaning grabbed from the air
to arrange in a beautiful bowl on the table.
Haven't you got a tongue in your head? Barks the man.
Language is a tool, like a hammer,
that can build a table or smash a skull;
they are arguing. I can see it from here:
he is laying it on thick, an impasto of lies
applied with the palate knife of his palm.
She rejects him with a single finger and a look;
for a moment she is speaking my language.
I spell a word for her with slow fingertips
and she laughs with a sound like gunfire.
I see my mistake: a handcrafted typo,
the kind that might get me into trouble
or, on the other hand, might make me a friend.

Island

Davide Malouf

OUT OF SIGHT

Painting the walls yellow was one way
of arriving in Sydney. I did it
via Brisbane and Birkenhead in '68, and the walls of
that room, stoked like the sun, were for two years my harbour
     view,
          their surrogate
hum, the way the light bounced off them
like water or water music more an extended
mood than a space to work in,
a place where I forgot
to be happy because I was.

Grace notes. Promissory
glimpses. Could paradise
be a colour? Can
music, the smell of cooking
from someone else's kitchen, table
set and the guests assembled, lead us there?
Or oxygen? Or prayer? In the free time being
of grace notes a yellow
wall blooms, a full sail pumped with sunlight, the clamorous
     swell

and pour it is making for still out
of sight, out of earshot.

_____

Heat

KATE MIDDLETON

YOUR FEET / LOVE POEM

Your undressed feet tell the story of my heart:
the lines troughs I could dip my hands into
to quench myself, the roughness of the nails,
dirty, and slightly squared, my roughness.

She was his model and his lover
(though I am unsure which role came first)
and from him she learned the trick of it —
later photographing the feet most revealingly.

My life is told in their naked surface.
So rarely bare they become for an instant the one
true thing: like an individually carved button,
the most sour lemon, the unbalancing abstention

of your hand. This photograph
was the most personal — no face, the identity
told in the skin knotted by work, and the simplicity
of sandals. There is nothing dainty in them.

Just like there is nothing dainty in your feet.
They are browner than mine could ever be

from time spent north. A beautiful code — the language
of everything I'll never know of you.

You have touched my own feet before, with hands
infinitely warmer, in the morning as we took flight
out of winter. Your hands rested on them
and later on my belly, a lover's fingers

laced into fear. My muteness a protestation
not of the way you thought my stomach smooth
but of the difference between us. How can I say it?
Your feet, bare with nothing like the relish

of my own. Your feet. Which I have never held.

Australian Book Review

GRAEME MILES

THE ROAD IN THE REAR-VIEW MIRROR AT NIGHT

is sad as an abandoned toy,
is transit distilled
with no claim to placehood
except the *ad hoc* shrines
where the cars squealed.
At night in the rear-view mirror the road
appears in quick bites
like political argument
vacant as a concrete stairwell.
In the rear-view mirror at night the road
looms on you
like the Homeric future in prophecy's double-talk.
It strobes through the present and past in front:
wheels, armour and bitumen
both sides of the mirror.

Blue Dog: Australian Poetry

LES MURRAY

THROUGH THE LATTICE DOOR

This house, in lattice to the eaves,
diagonals tacked across diagonals,

is cool as a bottle in wicker.
The sun, through stiff lozenge leaves,

prints verandahs in yellow Argyle.
Under human weight, the aged floorboards

are subtly joined, and walk with you;
French windows along them flicker.

In this former hospital's painted wards
lamplit crises have powdered to grief.

Inner walling, worn back to lead-blue,
stays moveless as the one person still

living here stands up from reading,
the one who returned here from her life,

up steps, inside the guesswork walls,
since in there love for her had persisted.

Quadrant

TED NIELSEN

PAX ROMANA

i.

under a strange head the visions line up
for stamps & approval, repeating your forebears
like a reflex (travel/statue/history/bingo!)
    while lunch burns.
you bet we're grateful then after dinner
the endless walking & wondering about
how to think of labour & sex as your arse
    starts to melt into the vista
    & your syntax contradicts itself/
another tram rumbling to a halt in a pile of fiats.

onset of tuberculosis? brilliant/surreptitious
digging in the protestant cemetery
& when australia beckons
you can miss the plane, departures revised
& the amused voice of the reservations clerk
extending assistance in the language you fashion
    like a club.

ii.

dodging the collected works of piaggio
up & down the via del corso

on the fag end of an 8 hour monument binge,
your feet impressed by weathered marble,
each pat reaction second-guessed
like a legion of american tourists thrilled
by fat, bored gladiators smoking at the colosseo
when all you want is a dancing topolino
& your own tabacchi, the sun setting
over acres of pizzeria & the remnants of empires.

iii.
is italy wasted on the flippant? streets of venezia's
grime & tack then intercity direct to roma,
coin purse empty at the trevi fountain.

trying to balance euro-disdain (nostalgia for the past
you never had) with another limonelli biscuit —
but are you social nexus or cultural interstice?
That's the type of question the tour guides
won't answer, & anyway, who's asking?

italian graffiti decorates the platform/alfa romeo the sky.
autostrada a kind of futurist squiggle on the country
you traverse sottopassaggio —
                                        another hilltop,
another stone ruin/agriculture's thrilling banality.

tuscan fantasy cancelled by inclement weather/
three day mosquito frenzy in the hotel byron

(no documentary evidence) & the lives of the saints
queuing for your travel dollar, rooms of art
& after those, more rooms, more art, more rooms,
    et cetera.

iv.

disconnected expatriate shambling
    through dirty rain,
the different light you try to see
escapes you & only travelogue remains,
christen's riff on tourism jangling the coins
in your hip pocket, candy coloured jacket
to signify difference/your body apes the local gape.

v.

vacant piazzas & the san sebastian
commemorative pincushion guide you,
the abstract of home kissing your sundried lips.
where is desire? to what end? jupiter nursed
by the goat amalthea or mercury
cooling his winged heels at the trenitalia
    ticketing counter.

a dog-eared copy of what god is that
& the all day breakfast courtesy of

insert name of company/glossolalia redux,
embracing the infinite vespa.

you stay up late & start the fresco,
coffee hissing in the pot.

Meanjin

Π . O .

THE PLATYPUS

from 'The Everything Poem' (part IV)

I feel like an axolotl.
'Who Goes There?' was the name of a novel.
/
'plonk!'
:the sound of a bottle
…
(Imagine breeding —- an OYSTER the size of a BED)

NOTE: It's the right
not the left hand side of the brain
that produces all those uncontrollable voices
you hear

Spread your fingers Out now
(infront of your face) (and don't count on the cost of
the advice *or salt*
in 1945
Lance Hill invented
the Hills Hoist
"''/''"

              L;o*-0)k a-t% !all
                      + [tH+…………issssSs]
       +ss-T\u;f+ -++++++!*++++;+ =f+#ing
Shakespeare used 719 full stops (and Charles Blondin once
              cooked an omelette [standing up] over
                      Niagara Falls)
tHi-s)))))sssss/sE-nTencE is, /+*+#! b/U;'s-t+*i/N-g
                      (with punctuation)

              A buccaneer's archipelago.
A canoe   (to Sumatra)
              A storm!))))
                      Gargoyles
                              were first used
                      as 'spouts'

                      : —

       to push rain-water *coming down off rooftops*
              away from a building
                      /
              some
                      diving-birds
only catch fish ———————————————————
              on the w-ing

                      !

So, who am I?!

A problem? (With a central nervous-system?)

(Or a scratch?)

(With a sound at the end of it?) Who Knows?!

In central South America

they've got a fish with 4 eyes — and another

that can turn itself

inside out

/

. . . .

(((((still)))))

unreality is what's woven

into the fabric; so don't die before you get

to MAYFAIR

:tuna belongs

to the mackerel family, and tomatoes

are rich

in potassium

HERE ARE THE RULES:

— pumpkins have sex

— cats purr at 25 vibrations a second

— fennel is good for the eye-brows

and an EGG

can be frozen

for up to 9 months

[Now]

I know a rehearsal

is a '*harrowing experience*', and that they turn

Niagara Falls *off*

at night

but the human-heart is about the *size* of a clenched fist

and *red-rain*

fell on England

in 1835

so scramble the message

[and *twiddle* the dial]

or you may find yourself locked-Up [in

a room] [all alone]

'neighing'

[like a horse]

/

periscopes are useful

for optically moving the eyes

around

Heat

PETER ROSE

U-BAHN

They are not cannibalising yet,
those lowered voices.
A sidelong glance out of Dürer
perfects the new vocation, a bitter tense.
Faces pressed too closely
as in a holy family skirmish
avert their gaze,
sepiaed and equivocal.
The Italian boy who is all lash
whispers in a foreign sleep.

Meanjin

BRENDAN RYAN

THE PADDOCK WITH THE BIG TREE IN IT

Like an anchor rattling overboard
she turns from her mother
heaving the morning into the spin dryer
and faces the paddocks.
The smell of mud is nesting in her head.
The tractor thundering in the shed
is pulling her around.
She walks like a dancer seasoned by grief
through the cow shit on the driveway.
All sorrows are accepted
as she divides the fence wires
her pilgrim legs splayed between the paddocks
between someone buzzing the bone
and someone licking the spoon,
between the bed she warms with her sisters
and the milking a girl should never do.
She drags her rubber boots through cape weed
stands in drains to watch dirty water rise.
Like an echo she returns
to the trunk of a dead gum tree

rubbed smooth by cows' necks.
She leans into wood
electrified as prayer.

Island

Margaret Scott

LAND

As the plane climbs she sees the separate places
in her life — streets and parks, the bush beyond the town,
a grid of paddocks, beaches edged with foam —
spread out as one, a realm, a land like those
in story books and hymns she used to sing
where some poor widow's son might save the king
from monstrous perils and win his daughter's hand;
the Spanish find undreamed-of stores of gold;
or saints immortal dwell in pure delight.
Cars bowl along the country roads like beads,
dams twinkle in the sun like scattered coins,
while all around the hills sit patiently,
their shoulders wrapped in capes of fleecy trees.
And far away — two, three days march at least —
one peak still white with snow burns unconsumed
as though a traveller here might chart a course
and know where in the end his feet would lead.

The Australian

KERRY SCUFFINS

YOUR HOUSE

Your handwriting
your books
your pad   unfilled
your empty chair
this quiet, quiet air

Never before would Satchmo
have sung in this room
at this hour

I can hear shooters in the forest
but I can't hear you say
Oh no. The bloody —

Aren't they Dad
those killers
in one form
or another
aren't they everywhere

Blue Dog: Australian Poetry

TOM SHAPCOTT

TOTEMS

(for Coral Hull)

I

We don't choose our own totem
it is something given.
Recognition does not follow
but there is a point
when you know it.
I could say
'It has descended on you'
but there isn't the taste.
The taste is that
you have always been aware.
You have to grow
to acknowledge just about everything.
Your totem
recognises you.

II

A tree
I would have thought
and there are many
in their separation.

I would have claimed
Toona Australis, I think:
Australian Red Cedar.
A legend in itself
and a timber
so beautiful my destructiveness
knew no bounds.
At one stage my house
was its Mausoleum.

III

Or Castanospermum Australis
the native Black bean.
The tree by our back fence
looking downhill
was everything shade invokes
in a hot climate and in its season
each arm and limb flowered
within that shade like bodysweat
but with gold red and soft syrups
that brought the greenleeks
shouting and plunging
deadset for the festival.
A kingfisher nested there
until our neighbour
hacked the tree down.

I V

Yes, a tree,
I thought.
The bark spiders waited.
I shuddered
perhaps sensing
even then
their time would come.
Feet soft as the undersides of leaves
and a quickness like bird-shadow
they remain
foreign
not to be understood
even when they are predictable.
They return
in my dreams
and I come home
to them
warily
— as befits a true Totem.

Blue Dog: Australian Poetry

MAGGIE SHAPLEY

EVIDENCE

The proof is in a single strand of hair:
that is all that's needed to lay the blame,
to name the father, victim or the thief
who tried to leave no fingerprints behind.

The doctor plucked a hair out of my daughter's
unborn head and held it up in tweezers.
'It's a girl' he said, his party-trick, certain
of scientific truth in the midwives' tale.

The white one's my mother's under glass,
the DNA extract shows the fatal gene
for predisposition, grim legacy
for four daughters, and seven more of theirs.

And this hair, blonde from root to tip, lying
on the ensuite floor, not mine or his,
tells another story —
no science to it, just the age-old truth.

Westerly

IAN C. SMITH

KEYS

He slammed the car door and realised, peering
in, knowing he had committed a breach,
at his keys dangling behind the steering
wheel, stranded like memory beyond reach,
he was locked out. He had been scheming to
abandon his family so he felt
agitated. He bashed without a clue
on the window, tried each door, even knelt
like a penitent to squint through the gap
where the door had closed although he knew this
was mad. His wife had guessed, her face a map
of despair. She begged and cursed, tried to kiss
his feet. He hurried away, no tears shed.
While bystanders stared he looked straight ahead.

Quadrant

Vivian Smith

HAPPINESS

They tell me that the novelist next door
is working on a new book full of fight
with all the characters named after colours:
Rose and Pink and Black and Brown and White.
He's the kind of guy who knows the ropes.
He is so at home in his own skin.
(Of course it could turn out a load of shite).

And I, today, have reached a small peak
of cloudless unconcern,
with no demands, and no calls on my time.

I'm standing at the window with a coffee,
the first flush of spring on view.
I know that in an hour you will return
and I will have this greeting right for you.

Heat

NORMAN TALBOT

SEVEN NEW SOUTH WALES
SONNET-FORMS

1   THE BAT, GUNNEDAH

All dust, from the old wicket out to the fences.
    Though hoof prints last in the tesserae of the dam
the cattle are gone, down the long paddock somewhere.
    Dust, thin along the smooth waterskin of the trough.

How can you smell the dust in this motionless air?
    Flies, once the voice of dust on all the dry senses,
have given up their sour whinge, 'I am that I am'.
    From the barn comes an old & air-dry human cough.

The shines gone off the leathery sun in the west;
    air darkens under these verandahs; dark feels good.
A straight-backed grey woman, breath crackling in her chest,
    bends over a sports-bag — its stiff straps won't uncoil —
lifts out by its handle a glisten of pale wood,
    the lost-world enchanted perfume of linseed oil.

2   THE CLARENCE AT GRAFTON

    Night. The train's gone as far
as it goes, & the town lights blink, sedate

north of a black-brown slab of river.
On the two-level bridge damp with late-
        fallen rain I walk the aimless dark …
Occasional splashy swoosh of a car
        over my right shoulder, yellow diffident blur
to show where the bridge steps down to a park.

Halfway across I look up … Up … & up.
        The high world is changed where a greylocked cloud
stumbles drunkenly aside from the moon.
        Curded with silver its water-furls droop.
The Clarence flows vast, scrawled with fools-gold runes.
        Read it sideways to everything ever made.

3 WARRAGAMBA DAM: THE TURN

— or volta, in sonnets. The story paces
through its long half, then takes a lover's leap
to its big end. The hourglass meaning-trap —
        but voltas are (if you look closely) spaces.

        Blank paper could be wisdom? Typical!
Wisdom in sonnets? That's fourteen bad years'
luck: octave ponded, volta a dam (sheer,
        with generators), sestet a trickle.

        A volta's not believable without
the churning water in spate at the climax.
Electric light decks whole suburbs of duplex

in 'vales' where Maribungo tickled trout,

Trained sonnets machine couplets to clinch matters.
'Yeah, & then what?' the primal spirit mutters.

4   SUBURBAN BEAST-FABLE

Postured tall, easy-smiling, regular
        dog in his flash slimwaist suit
makes a deposit (& a solid one) on

        a desirable subdiv
of our lawn; no legals, no duty. Done!
        Kicks on, lifts his back elbow

to exchange car contracts, above-board,
(special discount on one wheel).

Obviously unemployed, these bludgers —
        our at best blue-collar cats —
slip warily around the back.

        Black economy for them:
no-one's supposed to see their private deals.
        On the quiet. Used notes. Dig?

5   THE BUSH YARN

An Irishman, a Scotsman, and a golden retriever
        all day in this outback pub, see, supping ale.

At dusk the Irishman has to go out the back:
　　　　the proverbial dunny at the end of the paddock.

He gets turned around. No pub! The track he'd followed
　　　　thins. It's getting dark, with rain. No house for miles …
Maybe he should've looked in kilometres?
　　　　Then a little light flickers, way off the road.

He goes up to this clapboard shack & knocks (he's soaked).
　　　　An old man peers out. 'Lost, are ye, Pat? Well, lad,
　　　　　　s'pose I can let yer in, but we've no grub for ye,
　　　　& if ye want to doss down ye'll have to share a bed
　　　　　　with me eldest son.' Pat turns with dignity away:
　　　　'Bedad! Dat's t'ree times I've got stuck in de wrong
　　　　　　joke!'

6 MARE

'Shiv' (Zhivotnikh), broad, shrewd blade-grey brood-mare
　　　　She stamps & swishes, nostrils wide & hot;
sniffing hard against her own hindquarters,
she celebrate herself & breathes herself.

　　　　Her trimmed hoofs dance their wisdom on the spot;
wisdom of smells that are, we tell ourselves,
beyond the tongue in a male human head …
　　　　'Watch out!' We both hiss. 'Up! Up on that rail!'

　　　　A vast golden spray of Shiv's piss-water
rattles & hisses through the new-spread straw

that had carried its own frail drying scents.

Both of us humans were up on the fence

at the first tense-&-arch of her tough tail:

   'She's do that, eh. Soon as I get it spread.'

7   READING BLAKE IN THE BUSH

The tygers of wrath are wiser than the horses of instruction
— WILLIAM BLAKE

Blake only saw town horses wearing bits,

   schooled to heave in shafts or under

milady's trim-clad bottom or between

   some rich fellow's shone well-heeled boots

not the young wild bristle-mane colts who'd run

   races with their shadows & win,

who lipped ripe apples off my open hand

   & crunched them with fantastic grins …

Those young art-dodgers ever on tiptoe,

   who'd snort panic-pollen, who'd see

afreets, who'd flee their own unshod thunder!

   Dancing loonies I used to know —

so uninstructed they thought themselves free …

   Yes, & free, so fierce their wonder!

Five Bells

97

JOHN TRANTER

BATS

In a freezing attic somewhere in Prague
a hungry songwriter invents Sincerity, but alas,
too early. A decade later, a popular singer,
struck by the intimacy a microphone fakes,
invents a way of sobbing in time to the music —
earnest little hearts are wrecked
from San Jose to Surbiton. The angelic
choirs, should they be tempted to rebel,

would they hit on a trick so lucrative? Clouds
of butterflies reassure us: we are so much more
serious, and intelligent — think of rockets, and
the invention of dentistry and napalm. Sincerity?
It will take a Poet Laureate to turn it to profitable use.
Bats circle the Old City, low and silent.

The Sydney Morning Herald

CHRIS WALLACE-CRABBE

OUR BIRTH IS BUT A SLEEP AND A FORGETTING

The man who believed
that televised weather forecasts
make it all happen:

the woman who did all her foreign travel
under a lemon tree
in her backyard, with an atlas:

the young man, faintly adventurous
who entered a maze and never came out,
leaving half a handkerchief behind:

the cabin attendant, or trolley-dolly,
afflicted by her entirely terrible
fear of heights:

the country butcher
whose father falling blind drunk
had been gobbled up by pigs:

the teenage girl whose main belief was
that, if she fell asleep, her legs
and arms could easily drop off:

the little boy who felt at night
the surrounding darkness
was all made of water:

and the chubby rose-pink baby
who had remembered it all
but now forgot.

Eureka Street

LINDA WESTE

HELDENTOD

(Lee Krasner recalls Jackson Pollock)

You were blown off: fingering jazz;
a percussive shatter of glass;
the horn's sudden fanfare;
spare steel's improvised notes.

The forgery of that sordid *mise en scène*:
love's undiscerning engine still warm.
If there was regret, it lay prostrate,
limp, and mute as a worm.

Yet, who could imitate the lyrical squirt,
the lava spill, the loop-the-loop, the tadpole spurt,
the spidery tics?

Each improper hybrid had a grace —
that defied the awkwardness of your fist,
the wildness manifest in your face.
Who else could resist measure from yardsticks?

From the frontier that is you, they wanted to
carve chunks the size of Iowa and Wyoming;

across unseen lands they came itching
to shake your Californian Redwood wrested hands.

With a backhand of contempt,
I've chased reductive myth and all its unkempt
accomplices: tried to keep you on the top shelf.
But now the idea of a definitive Pollock
will have to fend for itself.

Laconic cowboy, who cares if you can't ride?
Just toss your lariats of paint across a great Western range of
      sky.

Salt-lick New Poetry

CONTRIBUTORS' NOTES

ROBERT ADAMSON lives on the Hawkesbury River, New South Wales with his partner, the photographer Juno Gemes, where he writes full-time. His latest publications are *Mulberry Leaves: Selected Poems 1970–2001* and *Reading the River* (Bloodaxe UK, 2004). Adamson's autobiography, *Inside Out*, was published in March, 2004 by Text Publishing (Melbourne).

Adamson writes: 'I wrote "Flag-Tailed Bird of Paradise" in a mood of rage, frustration and sadness. War is such an old-fashioned way of dealing with anything. Victory in relation to so much carnage (physical and spiritual) is hollow and it solves nothing in the long run; the only thing that continues after war is the suffering of the victims and their loved ones.'

ADAM AITKEN has published five collections of poetry. The fourth, *Romeo and Juliet in Subtitles*, was shortlisted for both the John Bray Award for Poetry and the Age Book of the Year Awards. His most recent book is *Impermanence.com* (Vagabond Press). He is completing a novel as part of a Doctorate in Creative Arts at the University of Technology, Sydney.

About 'At Batu Caves, Kuala Lumpur' Aitken writes: 'Batu Caves is a famous limestone outcrop in Kuala Lumpur. The cave once served the British and then the Japanese armies as their ammunition dump in WW2. It is now an important centre of Hindu worship for Malaysia's Indian community, and a popular tourist destination. I was a visitor there in 1998 when I was an Asialink writer-in-residence. Despite the freeway that sweeps past its gates, the site resists the sanitising drive of modernity. Always more than a mere spectacle, it remains for me a sacred but utterly human space.'

ERIC BEACH was born in New Zealand on 21 October, 1947, and he came to Australia on 9 February, 1972. His poetry has won The Age Book of the Year (for poetry) and the New South Wales Premier's Prize for Poetry. He also writes for actors and musicians. He lives in the Wimmera.

Beach writes: '"Wimmera Easter Sunday" was written on that day, 2003. I'd been working on a book of poems for my partner Judith St Leger who died of motor neurone disease (ALS). I've rewritten these poems so many times that they overlap like scales. Times hard to face and relive. I wrote this poem for myself in anger and frustration. I wrote it a line or two at a time and hardly changed a line except to run events together as memories jump to different keys. Why did I keep it? It's a kaleidoscope of hurts, a litany petitioning unjust fate. Love's not mentioned but it's tangled there. In rewriting it I considered it as a piece, how it builds musically within a conversational tone.'

JUDITH BEVERIDGE was born in England in 1956 and came to Australia in 1960. She has published three books of poetry, *The Domesticity of Giraffes* (Black Lightning Press, 1987), *Accidental Grace* (UQP, 1996) and *Wolf Notes* (Giramondo, 2003), and has also co-edited an anthology of Australian poetry, *A Parachute of Blue* (Round Table Publications, 1996). Her work has also been translated into several languages and has been set for HSC study.

About 'Appaloosa' Beveridge writes: 'I don't as a rule set myself writing tasks, but when I read David St John's poem "Guitar" whose opening line is "I have always loved the word *guitar*," I thought I'd try a similar approach. I have in fact always loved the word "appaloosa" — but as to why I chose that particular word from a field of many, I'm not sure, other than the fact that I knew the poem would need something very concrete to work with. I love naming things, so this poem allowed me the joy of doing just that, and as a result I think it endeavours to say something about the elemental pleasure of words.'

ELIZABETH BLACKMORE was born, raised, educated and commenced a teaching career in Melbourne. She has a Master of Arts Degree (Literature) from Macquarie University and a Graduate Diploma in Community Counselling from University of Canberra. She spent many years teaching in Sydney, Rural NSW, and the ACT in secondary schools, TAFE, CIT, and the Prison System. She has been a sometime opal miner, sheep farmer, travelling salesperson and house renovator, and she currently lives and works on the far South Coast of NSW.

Of 'Dog Bite' Blackmore writes: 'I think the poem reflects my surprise that my lovely, loyal and non-aggressive kelpie, Lady, actually bit me. I had grabbed her out of a dog fight and thought that I was holding her out of reach of the other dog, but unbeknownst to me, it was gnawing at her hind leg. She bit me so that she could get free and defend herself. At the hospital the dictum that if a dog bites it is put down was reflected in the doctor's question. Given the physical reaction of shock and the severity of the bite, I felt unable to defend my dog's action. Lady died three years ago at twenty years of age after years as a mediocre sheep dog but a very good companion. The scar on my forearm is the perfect horseshoe shape of her mouth with the two canine teeth marks, and their stitches like stars on the underneath. Every time I notice these marks I think of her with love. The last line of the poem tempers the serious tone and indicates acceptance of the incident as one of life's happenings.'

JANICE BOSTOK is an internationally award-winning haiku poet, but also writes other Japanese forms and free verse. Her first collection, *On Sparse Brush*, was one of the Gargoyle Poets Series from Makar Press (1978). Since then her haiku seem to have become more popular than her free verse, although her free verse is being published in a number of print and online magazines. She is looking forward to a second collection of free verse in 2004.

Bostok writes: '"The Widow" is one of those poems which begins in reality but leads the creative mind down a number of pathways. I heard of a woman whose husband died and she spent all his money, almost immediately. It was rumoured that one expensive item was a face-lift! One day I noticed a "poor" widow wearing what seemed to be a second-hand skivvy and she kept putting two fingers into the neckline and stretching it out as if it was choking her. As I have also spent time breeding dogs, I transferred the action of the two-finger-width between collar and dog to the poem. So while the poem was inspired by a true experience, the Widow took off in my mind and began a life of her own.'

PETER BOYLE and MTC CRONIN. Boyle was born in Melbourne in 1951. His three collections of poetry have received many honours including the Kenneth Slessor Prize for Poetry; two National Book Council Awards; and the John Bray Award for Poetry from the Adelaide Festival. He has translated extensively from French and Spanish poets, notably Lorca, Vallejo, Pierre Reverdy and, most recently, the Venezuelan poet Eugenio Montejo. His most recent collection is *Museum of Space* (UQP, 2004). Cronin has published six books and three booklets of poetry, the most recent being *beautiful, unfinished ~ parable/song/canto/ poem* (Salt UK, 2003). Her 2001 book, *Talking to Neruda's Questions,* is being translated into Spanish by the poet, Juan Garrido Salgado, and a collection of her work is being translated into Bosnian by Tatjana Lukic. She is currently working on her doctorate, *The Law of Love Letters ~ Prose, Poems, Law & Desire,* at UTS. Her next book, *<more or Less Than 1–100>*, is forthcoming in September, 2004 (Shearsman UK).

About 'Objects of You in Water' Boyle and Cronin write: 'The idea of trying to write a collaborative poem came partly from the example of the Octavio Paz-Charles Tomlinson collaboration: "Hijos del Aire / Airborn" where Paz and Tomlinson, having agreed on a theme that seemed to be central to both their work, wrote a series of linked sonnets in which one would begin with a stanza and the other continue with a matching stanza. We had in mind a much looser arrangement wherein one of us would start with a line, several lines or a stanza, and the other would build onto that and so on until one or both of us felt a natural ending had been reached. Very soon in the process, two themes seemed to take over the poems: the act of writing, especially the act of writing poetry; and love — the gamut of emotions, needs, inadequacies summoned by that word. More specifically there gradually arose in the work a sense of unique spaces: domestic or watery: and of landscapes with a special resonance — the house, the urban skyline, the ocean. As the poems went back and forth over emails they seemed to find their own directions and prompt new responses. The writing of the collaborative poem was an exciting process: it seemed to free up the imagination and push us both forward to construct poems different from what either of us might have attempted alone. This is because the joint work forms itself through another kind of "longing"; a searching for "an other" that is in actuality present in the poem-making process.'

ELIZABETH CAMPBELL was born, lives, writes, sings and plays with horses in Melbourne.

Campbell writes: 'The Tremulous Hand is the name given by scholars to an anonymous scribe of the thirteenth century, probably a monk, who lived and worked at Worcester Cathedral. His handwriting is distinctive in its marked tremor. The scribe was also a scholar who made a long study of Old English, glossing OE manuscripts in Middle English and Latin. We know nothing about him except what can be gleaned from his glosses. I first came across his beautiful, metonymic name while researching a popular late medieval literary genre, the "soul-body dialogue." One of the manuscripts the scribe copied was a precursor to this genre. I am fascinated by his unknown life, devoted to scholarship and, presumably, God, and working with what was most probably a congenital tremor. I am working on a collection of poems which will take its title from this one — "Letters to the Tremulous Hand" — and this year I will travel to Worcester and Oxford to see some of the original manuscripts.'

LIDIJA CVETKOVIC was born in the former Yugoslavia in 1967 and came to Australia in 1980. After working as a teacher, she completed an Arts Degree at the University of Queensland and currently works as a psychologist in Brisbane. She has travelled widely in Europe and the Middle-East. Her first collection, *War Is Not the Season for Figs*, won the inaugural Arts Queensland Thomas Shapcott Poetry Prize and was published by UQP in 2004.

Cvetkovic writes: '"A Seed, a Crutch, a Heart" draws, in part, on wedding customs and practices from my homeland Serbia, where traditionally wedding celebrations take place over three days and cast family members into specific roles with the purpose of enlivening the proceedings with jokes and pranks. Many of the practices have their roots in pagan beliefs. In writing this poem I took on the role of one such prankster and embellished the proceedings with details drawn from my own experiences and from my imagination.'

LUKE DAVIES is the author of two novels, including the best-seller *Candy*, and five books of poetry, including *Running With Light*, winner of the Judith Wright Poetry Prize. *Candy* is in development as a film, to be directed by Neil Armfield. His work has been widely published both here and overseas, and translated into German, Spanish, Thai, French and Hebrew. His latest volume of poetry is *Totem* (Allen & Unwin, 2004). Davies is the recipient of the 2004 Philip Hodgins Memorial Medal for poetry.

About 'Totem Poem' Davies writes: 'The poem exploded upon me in Thailand in early 1999, where I was writer-in-residence at the Australia Centre in Chiang Mai. I knew almost immediately what its form would be. I wanted to try my hand at a giant poem bursting out of its skin and leaking, so to speak, an awful lot of juice … yet somehow still reined in and contained within a quite formal structure, a coherent metricality. I wanted to attempt an epic monologue of the essential impulse of love as it is experienced by the inner narrative self. I wanted to explore the interweaving of the vernacular and the mythical on an extended scale. I wanted to write a kind of biography of love, a paean to life, that was quite literally totemic: different animals would represent different stages in the journey of an imagination set in motion. I wanted to set loose a poem that enacted what Wylie Sypher calls the Baroque principle of expenditure, of giant mass in motion, in complete release, in dynamic fulfillment. Who knows how much I've succeeded with all that. But I like this poem. I didn't of course set out consciously with all those notions in hand; like I said, suddenly the poem was there, taking shape. After that, it took the next four or five years to build the structure up, get it right. It wasn't the sole thing I was working on but probably it took up the most psychic space.'

BRUCE DAWE, widely recognised as Australia's most popular poet, was born in Fitzroy, Victoria in 1930. He worked in a variety of occupations before retiring from the University of Southern Queensland in 1992 when he was appointed their first Honorary Professor. After successfully completing two Masters degrees and a PhD, he was awarded honorary degrees from the University of Southern Queensland and the University of New South Wales. Other awards include the Grace Leven Poetry Prize (1978), the Patrick White Literary Award (1980), the Order of Australia (AO) for his contribution to Australian literature (1992), the inaugural Philip Hodgins Medal for Literary Excellence (1997), and the Australia Council Arts Emeritus Writers Award for his long and outstanding contribution to Australian literature (2000). Dawe has published thirteen books of poetry, a book of short stories, a book of essays, and three children's books (Penguin). His collected edition *Sometimes Gladness* (Longman, 1997) was named by the National Book Council as one of the ten best books published in Australia in the previous decade.

Dawe writes: '"Annie" is from *The Headlong Traffic* (Longman, 2003). While my wife, Liz, was doing some family research she discovered that I had another sister who died shortly after birth and before I was born.'

JAN DEAN, a former visual arts teacher, returned to poetry in 1996. She lives at Cardiff, Lake Macquarie. In 1999 she became the first woman President of Poetry at the Pub, Newcastle. She won the 2001 NSW Women Writers' Open Poetry Award and was placed second in the 2002 Arts Queensland Val Vallis Award. Her work has won and been placed in numerous competitions, translated into Arabic and published in journals, newspapers and anthologies.

Dean writes: '"Signed Auguste Rodin" is a response to Louise Waller's imaginative and sensuous "Such" with an epigraph by Rodin in *Blue Dog* 1.2. Although this is a "one-off" I love the idea of an ongoing poetic correspondence through journals. Inhabiting Rodin enabled my celebration of his radical approach to surface and the fleeting moment — a sculptural counterpart of impressionist painting — through bronze editions. Rainer Maria Rilke, who was Rodin's secretary for a time, wrote *Dinggedichte* or "thing-poems," some of which capture the life within carved animals in Rodin's studio: my concerns are the human form and psyche.'

TIM DENOON is a Sydney poet whose work has appeared invarious Australian and international journals. He is currently working on his first novel.

Denoon writes: 'The poem "Clovelly" was written in the most unlikely of places: dusty, dazzling, deafening Delhi. Being away from my foreshore home seemed to magnify the memory of a recent break-up — the frosted water, the inscrutable groper and a painfully bright pair of Speedos. Later when I returned to Sydney I discovered that a diver with a speargun had lanced the groper and walked off through the sunbathers with the magnificent trophy dragging at his feet. I often think what accursed luck it is that beautiful poems will most likely be born from such bitterness.'

DAN DISNEY recently completed his first collection of poems, *machina*, during a residency at Yaddo. He is currently travelling from Morocco to India and will begin a PhD when he returns to Australia. He is the recipient of the 2004 Somerset National Poetry Prize.

About 'Ecce Hombre' Disney writes: 'If poems are speaking pictures then this poem spoke suddenly, screeching like a television switched on in a dark room. I probably wrote it on a Tuesday, the day I usually write my first drafts, though the title (approximately: "behold the dude") had arrived weeks earlier. "Ecce Hombre" attempts to behold the dude — dialectical, manic, able to sense moments of the sublime (which I get the sense probably won't change much for any of them).'

LAURIE DUGGAN lives in Brisbane and has published eleven books of poems, most recently *Mangroves* (UQP, 2003) which won the 2003 Age Poetry Book of the Year award. He is an Honorary Research Advisor in the Centre for Australian Studies at the University of Queensland and is also the author of *Ghost Nation: Imagined Space and Australian Visual Culture, 1901–1939* (UQP, 2001).

Duggan writes: '"British Columbia Field Notes," as its title implies, is an example of a kind of thing I do that could be characterised as "cultural anthropology" (if I wanted to be unkind about it I could use Pam Brown's term and call it a "747 poem," i.e. an example of a poet bungee-jumping into a foreign country and writing a poem about his or her experience the next week). I don't see the poem as being necessarily illuminating, nor do I regard myself as an instant Canada expert. Instead I play a little with the ridiculousness of the anthropological role and the idea that what I say will be "taken notice of." "BC Field Notes" is an equivalent of *cinema verité*, a kind of hand-held-camera piece that attempts to explain itself through digression. The events and things described don't necessarily "add up" and the shape in the end is, I hope, the shape of a poem rather than a dissertation.'

CHRIS EDWARDS is the Sydney-based author of *utensils in a landscape* (Vagabond) and *A Fluke: A Mistranslation of Stéphane Mallarmé's 'Un coup de dés ...'* (Monogene).

About 'The Awful Truth' Edwards writes: 'Most of my poems are built around quotations, which I manipulate in various ways and piece together like collages. In this case, there was only one source: Richard Schikel's *Cary Grant: A Celebration*. I scanned this book at random, letting words and phrases disconnect themselves from it, rearrange themselves in my head and, interleaved with words of "my own," take shape as a poem. The result ("The Awful Truth"), named after a movie in which Cary Grant plays the male lead, is more about "patter," "pattern" and other portents than it is about the actor — the pseudonym or persona so memorably projected by Archibald Leach. It is, however, intended as a tribute to the "simple decency" and "consular good manners" that are the inimitable hallmarks of his style.'

LIAM FERNEY is an emerging Brisbane poet who has published widely in Australia, the United States, Canada and New Zealand. 'Angel' is from his first collection of poetry, *Popular Mechanics*. He is currently Poetry Editor at *Cordite* and Associate Editor at *papertiger*.

Ferney writes: '"Angel" is the story of two jewel thieves holed up in their hideaway somewhere in the hills of Los Angeles.'

KRIS HEMENSLEY, born in the UK in 1946, came to Melbourne in 1966 where, apart from three years in Southampton, '69–'72, and, since '87, regular return trips, he's lived ever since. A writer of poetry and prose, theatre & radio-plays, criticism and commentary, he has published several books & booklets & been anthologised. He edited his own little magazines between 1968 and 1986 (eg, *Our Glass, Earth Ship, The Ear in A Wheatfield*) and has been poetry editor for other small and mainstream magazines in Australia and England. He dropped out to be a poet in the '60s, then dropped out of the poetry scene to sustain his vocation in the '80s. A member of Collected Works Bookshop since 1984 and its coordinator since 1988, he has been happily in and out of publishing and public reading for a decade. He currently imagines publishing collections again.

Hemensley wrties: "'The Happiness of Winter" is from a 200+ sequence, "The Millennium Poems," written between 1997 and mid-2000. I wrote poems of varying type and length, often of my Melbourne locale — Westgarth by the Merri Creek, the City, and particular bus and train routes (where most of my writing is done, in a notebook, in transit). I wanted to catch the immediate present as well as referring to the literary past, to sponsor tradition against the tabula rasa fantasy the notion of "millennium" appeared to incite. For many years I've been troubled by a sense of being foreign to idiom, as though my British-English was echo-less in Australia. "The Happiness of Winter" is one of many poems grappling with this psychological and linguistic problem. A fretwork of simple rhymes carries the British sound into the Australian, deliberately merging poetic and colloquial. It's a poem of home-making and homecoming, one of my own favourites.

RAE DESMOND JONES was born in Broken Hill in 1941. From 1973 to 1981 he had four poetry books published. Three of these books were printed by Makar Press and one by The Saturday Centre, both sadly now defunct. In 1991, a novel *The Lemon*

Tree was published by Angus & Robertson in their imprint series. A further novel, *Wisdom*, was published by Blackwattle Press, which has also regrettably passed on. Since, he has written a further novel, *The Seven Gated City*, and a book of poems, *High Tide*. He is looking for publishers interested in either of these works. Over the last ten years he has been a local Councillor and, for one year, Deputy Mayor of his area.

About 'El Niño' Jones writes: 'The poem began as a meditation on the impact of a drought on my backyard. It transformed itself of its own volition into a semi-autobiographical recollection. Semi-autobiographical because, although the theme relates to my family, I have exaggerated some details and omitted others. I retained the original title at the end because it was curiously and ironically apt.'

AILEEN KELLY grew up in England, and is now an adult educator in Melbourne. Her first book, *Coming Up for Light*, won the Mary Gilmore Award and was shortlisted for the Anne Elder and the Victorian Premier's Poetry Awards. She is widely published in Australia, Ireland and elsewhere. Her latest book is *City and Stranger* (Five Islands, 2002).

About 'Mood / Tense' Kelly writes: 'As often happens, I fell into this poem accidentally. Someone was regretting that hardly anyone now uses the subjunctive, as an elegant way of implying "contingent," "not yet real." Next day I found myself saying of a friend afflicted with the indecision that can come with depression, "Of course she's moody, she's living in the subjunctive." (Puns come naturally to me, even when I'm being serious.) Grammar is an underlying "imagery" — changing the person, changing tense, using simple sentences or subordinating clauses, being passive or active: these decisions deeply alter the experience offered by a poem. Making the grammar an overt imagery and wordplay in this poem was fun, so it seemed a good idea to discipline it with the alternating nine and eleven syllable lines. It's a carefully structured poem on a serious subject, but I hope readers can also enjoy its verbal playfulness.'

EMMA LEW was born in Melbourne in 1962. Her first collection of poems, *The Wild Reply* (Black Pepper, 1997), won the Mary Gilmore Award and was joint-winner of The Age Poetry Book of the Year. Her second collection, *Anything the Landlord Touches* (Giramondo, 2002), won the Judith Wright Calanthe Award and the Victorian Premier's Prize for Poetry.

Lew writes: '"Sugared Path" was the first thing I wrote that seemed to work in over a year. It never felt like "writer's block," more an estrangement from poetry and the process of writing a poem. This one was the turning point: while working on it I became aware that the old sense of excitement and engagement was returning. I was trying for a tone of edginess, anger and confusion.'

KATHRYN LOMER was born in northwest Tasmania and now lives in Hobart. She studied literature and European languages as a mature-age student and became a teacher of English as a second language. She has worked in this capacity in Australia and Japan. She has written: a novel, *The god in the ink* (UQP, 2001) and a poetry collection, *Extraction of Arrows* (UQP, 2003), which was shortlisted for the Adelaide Festival Awards for Literature. Along with poetry, her short fiction has been published in a variety of Australian publications.

About 'On the Tongue' Lomer writes: 'Towards the end of 2002, I needed to have an operation on my tongue. I became intensely aware of the tongue's sensations and discovered a whole sensory memory to do with the tongue. Coincidentally, I came across an advertisement in a magazine at the hospital, a diagram of the tongue divided up like a butcher's poster of a side of beef. My head became crowded with tongue idioms. I was also very affected by the atmosphere of the hospital, the vulnerability one feels there and the way hospitals bring you down to earth and body with a resounding thump. The time of writing the poem was clouded by the rhetoric of impending war on Iraq, and I couldn't help but think of the wildly varying uses of language.'

DAVID MALOUF is a poet, essayist and fiction writer. He lives in Sydney.

About 'Out of Sight' Malouf writes: 'As often happens this poem started off as a vividly present sense impression in which colour became water became music. The first lines arrived all in a rush and were never changed. What they established as tone and rhythm determined the rest, though it took a little trouble, and several changes, to discover where the ideas they had set up were actually going.'

KATE MIDDLETON is a writer and musician. Her poems have previously appeared in many journals and newspapers including *ABR, Heat, Meanjin, Tinfish* (US), *The Age* and *The Australian*. She is currently completing an Arts/Music degree at the University of Melbourne.

About 'Your Feet / Love Poem' Middleton writes: 'This poem was written during a week of running barefoot in Adelaide. The photographer referred to is Tina Modotti — among her many moving photographs taken in Mexico during the early twentieth century is the portrait of a pair of feet, showing the wear and hardships of the peasant's life.

GRAEME MILES is a poet from Perth who is currently dividing his time between poetry and a PhD in ancient Greek literature at the University of Western Australia. He was recently Emerging Writer in Residence at the Peter Cowan Writers' Centre and has published work in various journals.

Miles writes: '"The Road in the Rear-View Mirror at Night" was written driving home from a German class on the far side of Perth's sprawl. Rewriting was pretty much finished off the next day. The closing lines about "the Homeric future" refer to the inverted (from our perspective) way of talking about past and future in early Greek. The past was thought of as in front, since it can be seen, while the future was behind, approaching invisibly. The Homeric character reverses into the future.'

LES MURRAY. The poems which Murray hasn't discarded from the first forty-odd years of his career are gathered in his *Collected Poems 1961–2002* (Duffy & Snellgrove, 2002). Other books by Murray include *Fredy Neptune* (verse novel, 1998); *A Working Forest* (selected prose, 1997); and *The Full Dress* (poems matched with works in The National Gallery of Australia, 2001). He has won major prizes in Australia, Britain and Germany, and his work has been published in seven European languages; further translations, into Hindi and Italian, are in progress.

About 'Through the Lattice Door' Murray writes: 'The owner of the lattice house wishes to preserve her privacy and doesn't want the location of her house revealed. It is fair to say that she seemed touched when I gave her a copy of my poem — but shortly afterwards, extensive renovations effaced the unpainted charm of decades and suppressed the old vivacity of the house's joinery.'

TED NIELSEN was born in Townsville, lived and worked in Sydney for a number of years, and from mid-2004 will be residing in Tokyo. His poems have appeared in a number of magazines and journals. His first book, *search engine*, was published by Five Islands Press and commended in the 1999 Anne Elder Award for Poetry. His second collection, *wet robot*, was published by Vagabond Press in 2001. His sequence 'townsville user's manual' was highly commended in the 2002 Josephine Ulrick Prize.

Nielsen writes: '"pax romana" is essentially travelogue, an awkward, impressionist collage arising out of generic European vacation. If you're feeling generous, you might flatter it by gesturing towards Walter Benjamin's figure of the flaneur, a wandering figure who attempts to observe without urgency, to explore without reaching conclusions. Is it possible to write poetry like this, or does it immediately dissolve into soundbites? ("is italy wasted on the flippant?"). I'm still not sure. It's possible to trace the route of a rough tourist's itinerary from the poem, although I don't know if the return would be worth the effort. But those movements are crucial to the poem, which tries to grapple with and draw energy from each detour, dislocation and mistranslation. The American artist Mike Kelly has said, "Too much is always expected of love and art," and yet you just have to keep trying, right? The last couplet is both metaphor and lie — there is no fresco — but you put the coffee on and stay up late because you hope there might be.'

Π.O. was born in Greece in 1951. Arrived in Australia 1955. Taken to Migrant Reception Centre at Bonegilla. Escaped three months later. Raised: Fitzroy! Sly grog gambling joints. Work as a Survey Draughtsman in the Titles Office and has done so for thirty-four years. Began writing poetry after seeing Johnny Cash on TV trying to read a poem. Edited *Fitzrot* magazine. Co-edited

925 magazine (worker's magazine "for the workers by the workers to the workers about the workers work"). Helped inaugurate the poets union and the advent of Performance Poetry in Australia. He is (philosophically) an Anarchist. Has been described as an oral-literate amongst other things. Did a sixteen-city tour of the USA in 1985. Edited *Off The Record* (an anthology of performance and visual poetry in Australia) with Penguin Books. Co-edited *Missing Forms* (an anthology of visual and concrete poetry in Australia, 1980). Co-wrote and performed in a play at the Sydney Wharf, *Call It Poetry Tonight* (1990). Represented Australia at the International Poetry Festival in Medellin Colombia 1998 and in 2003 the Berlin (Weltklang) Arts Festival. Has appeared on ABC TV and SBS a number of times. Did two documentaries on ABC Radio National in 1980 about the Migrant Riots at Bonegilla (in 1952 and 1961). Has just completed a biography of the Australian Dadaist poet Jas H. Duke: *Poems of Life And Death*. Books of poetry include: *Panash; The Fuck Poems; 24 Hours; The Fitzroy Poems;* and *The Number Poems*.

About 'The Platypus' Π.O. writes: 'The poem is composed of information that doesn't necessarily interrelate, just like the platypus which was seen as a freak of nature when it was first discovered by whites, i.e. composed of unrelated bits and pieces, eg a bit like a rat a bit like a duck a bit like a snake a bit like a fish etc etc.'

PETER ROSE grew up in country Victoria and went to Monash University. Throughout the 1990s he was the Publisher at Oxford University Press in Australia. He is currently the Editor of *Australian Book Review*. He has published three books of poetry, most recently *Donatello in Wangaratta* (1998). In 2001 he published the award-winning family memoir, *Rose Boys*. His poetry, reviews and journalism appear in various newspapers and magazines.

Of 'U-Bahn' Rose writes: 'The way we choose to travel can reflect the way we write poetry — and vice versa. Travel has a kind of poetry, after all, and poetry is all about crossings, embarkations and transmogrification. Many of us travel to get away from the known and from known selves; poetry beguiles us with its masked forms and foreign voices. Poetry, too, has its maps, its delays, its surprises, its decorum, its minor epiphanies. You board the wrong train, only to discover that it is the right one for you.'

BRENDAN RYAN was born in Warrnambool in 1963 and grew up on a dairy farm at Panmure in Victoria. His first collection of poetry, *Why I Am Not A Farmer*, was published by Five Islands Press in 2000. He lives in Portarlington.

Ryan writes: '"The Paddock with the Big Tree In It" was the first in a series of poems I wrote about the paddocks on my parents' farm. The series is titled "Naming the Paddocks." The impetus for writing the poems about the paddocks was to tap into the colloquial names farming families often give their paddocks, and then to subvert this general sense of naming the paddock into a more personal, emotional response to the characteristics of each paddock. Some of the paddocks in the series are described or written about more literally than others. The paddock referred to in the poem does actually have a large, craggy old pine tree on the boundary fence of the paddock and it also used to have a gum tree in its centre. However the gum tree has since died and been cut up for firewood. The female persona in the poem orginated from one of my sisters who used to walk up the paddock when she wanted to get away from her nine brothers and sisters and read books beneath the gum tree. Being the first poem in the series, "The Paddock with the Big Tree In It" was written quickly, with the tone of the female persona more or less driving the poem. It was an interesting exercise writing a poem to a title.'

MARGARET SCOTT was born in Bristol, England in 1934. After reading English at Cambridge she worked in a false eyelash factory, taught in two schools and in 1959 emigrated to Tasmania with her first husband and their sixteen-month-old son. Although she arrived determined to return to Britain after two years, she is now addicted to Tasmania and would not live anywhere else. For twenty-four years she taught in the English Department of the University of Tasmania, retiring in 1989 to become a full-time writer. Scott has written four books of poetry, two novels, a study of the Port Arthur Massacre and a semi-auto-biographical, *Changing Countries*. She has also written numerous articles, poems and short stories for periodicals in Australia, New Zealand, UK and the US. She is a well-known public speaker and has appeared in 'World Series' debates and the parodic quiz show 'Good News Week' on television.

Of 'Land' Scott writes: 'One day when flying out of Hobart I was startled to see dozens of places which I know separately all spread out in relation to each other. I then began to think about the enticing meanings of land, a word which seems to encompass a great range of meanings and mysteries. It occurs in hymns, fairy stories and travellers' tales.'

KERRY SCUFFINS was born in Canberra, grew up in Ballarat and has lived for many years in her favourite city, Melbourne. She has a son, Tom, aged seven who is her greatest creation and inspiration. She enjoys books, music, nature, animals and being a mum. She has had five collections of poetry published, and is working on a sixth, *Litmus*. 'Your House' is from *Prey*, her fifth collection.

About 'Your House' Scuffins writes: 'This poem is one of the poems for my father, who died suddenly when his car collided with a truck on his way to his weekly cards game. (These grief poems — for my daughter, my father and my step-daughter — make up the book *Prey*.) It is a simple poem, which I hope evokes a strong sense of absence, loss and change, written as it unfolded, late at night in the family home soon after my Dad's death.'

TOM SHAPCOTT was born in Ipswich in 1935, one of twins, and has lived in various cities in Australia and overseas. He currently lives in Melbourne but is Professor of Creative Writing at the University of Adelaide, so he is split between locations. His novel *Spirit Wrestlers* was published in 2004 and his chapbook of sonnets, *Beginnings & Endings*, came out with Picaro Press in 2003.

Of 'Totems' Shapcott writes: 'Yes, I am an arborist. I had been in correspondence with poet Coral Hull and perhaps her passion for animals made me realise that if I did have a personal totem (and why not?) it was the thing that I had always feared, not rejoiced in. It is a coming-to-terms poem and when I started it I did not quite know where it would end. It made a claim on me, not me on it.'

MAGGIE SHAPLEY works at the National Archives of Australia, and is editor of *Archives and Manuscripts*, the journal of the Australian Society of Archivists. She won the 2003 ACT Writers Centre Poetry Award and was shortlisted for the 2003 Arts ACT Poetry Award. She has a Master of Arts degree in early

English literature from the University of Sydney and lives in Canberra.

Shapley writes: 'The impetus for "Evidence" was a radio news item I heard in 1999: that scientists were able to detect from a person's hair if their DNA indicated a predisposition to develop cancer. I wrote in a notebook at the time: single strand of hair, evidence of crime, test for cancer, deadly inheritance, Mum — four daughters, nine granddaughters; me — two daughters. The poem resulting from that draft is about the nature of evidence, scientific or otherwise.'

IAN C. SMITH lives with his wife and their four sons in the Gippsland Lakes region. His poetry has been widely published in Australia and overseas, and his two collections of verse, *These Fugitive Days* and *This is Serious*, were published by the Ginninderra Press, both in 2003. 'Keys' was first published in *Quadrant* under the pseudonym 'S.M. Chianti.'

Of 'Keys' Smith writes: 'I used to write short fiction, and when I turned to poetry I think I liked the idea of writing narrative poems as an effective way of capturing the pathos of everyday life in as few words as possible. After reading the sonnets of the American poet Thomas Carper, I decided to write a series of narrative poems in that form. I know the idea for the "story" behind "Keys" came from something I read in bed but can't remember the book. That's when and where I scribbled the first drafts of "Keys" — in bed.'

VIVIAN SMITH was born in Hobart in 1933. He retired in 1996 from the University of Sydney where he spent over thirty years teaching in the Department of English. His many publications include *New Selected Poems* (1995) and *Late News* (2000). A new volume, *Along the Line*, is in preparation.

About 'Happiness' Smith writes: 'While some of my poems require quite long periods of drafting and reworking, this one seemed to arrive fully formed, and perhaps that was a part of the feeling of happiness I wished to capture. I like my poems to be formally complex but immediate and self-explanatory in content. The poem is addressed to the most important and most beautiful person I know, who has been a part of my life for nearly fifty years.'

NORMAN TALBOT, born and educated in England, came to a university lectureship in English at Newcastle, New South Wales in 1963, with his wife and first child. His later children were born in Newcastle. Apart from scholarly publications, Talbot is the author of eleven books of poetry (the first five published by South Head Press) and the editor of eighteen poetry anthologies. His *Four Zoas of Australia* (Paper Bark, 1992) was shortlisted for the National Book Awards and the Victorian Premier's Award; *The Book of Changes* (Nimrod, 1999), with forty-one full-colour pictures by John Montefiore, is still in the bookshops. His most recent collection *Every Sonnet Tells a Story* (Koel Koel, 2003) includes the sonnet sequence, 'Seven New South Wales Sonnet-Forms,' which won the 2002 Broadway Poetry Prize. As founder of Nimrod Publications, he has published approximately 400 writers from the Hunter Valley since 1964. Norman Talbot died suddenly on 8 January, 2004.

JOHN TRANTER has published twenty collections of poetry including *The Floor of Heaven*, a book-length sequence of four verse narratives (HarperCollins, 1992 and Arc UK, 2001), *Studio Moon* and *Trio* (both Salt UK, 2003). His work appears in the *Norton Anthology of Modern Poetry*. In 1992 he edited (with Philip Mead) the *Penguin Book of Modern Australian Poetry*, a

470-page anthology which has become the standard text in its field. He is the editor of the free Internet magazine, *Jacket*, at http://jacketmagazine.com.

Of 'Bats' Tranter writes: 'One day in the early sixties I had a vision or hallucination of a huge bird flapping over the skyline of Prague at dusk, a city I had not seen before. I finally made it there in 1999 to do a lecture at Charles University and a poetry reading at The Globe bookstore, but I didn't see any birds or bats, only a neatly beribboned pet goat being taken for a walk late one night. As for crying in time to the music, I must have had crooner Johnnie Ray (1927–1990) in mind: he had a huge hit with his lachrymose ditty "Cry," which had teenagers all over the world in floods of tears for months in 1951. He was partly deaf and bisexual, though we didn't know either of those facts at the time. There was also Guy Mitchell (born the same year, coincidentally the same year John Ashbery was born; died 1999) whose "Singing the Blues" was a big hit in 1957. It was a chirpy hillbilly number, about as much like the blues as "The Beer Barrel Polka," though in distant New South Wales we didn't know or care about things like that. It contained the immortal and ungrammatical lines, "There's nothing left for me to do / But crying over you," which was sung "cry-high-highin over you": a kind of rhythmically-synchronised sobbing.'

CHRIS WALLACE-CRABBE is Melbourne poet and art critic. He is also Professor Emeritus in the Australian Centre, University of Melbourne. His latest collection is *By and Large* (Brandl & Schlesinger / Carcanet), along with several artists' books.

About 'Our Birth Is But a Sleep and a Forgetting' Wallace-Crabbe writes: 'This piece is written against the grain of those earlier poems which gained their energy from the illogic of real or simulated dreams. At the same time its progress is cumulative: somewhere between "The Old Lady Who Swallowed a Fly" and Auden's "Law like Love." Its hinge works between our illusions and realities, but with some of the comedy of the Eastern European poets. I hesitated over the title (being a specialist in titles), but in the end went back to Wordsworth who was, despite his puddingy diction, the most profound psychologist in English poetry. Incidentally, this is a favourite poem of my youngest son, so it must have something to keep up with "The Simpsons." And it was enjoyable to write.'

LINDA WESTE is interested in themes that have been cross-pollinated by the Arts, particularly through music, the visual arts and literature. Recent work explores the 'voices' of characters to convey differing, or peripheral, perspectives. Writing in progress currently includes a contemporary version of a 15th century French (Parisian) poem cycle, *danse macabre des femmes*.

Of 'Heldentod' Weste writes: 'Pollock was an appealing subject for a "personae" poem. I'd read that Lee Krasner, his wife and fellow artist, had said, "I have so many myths about him to fight, I feel I must at last speak up," and that was my starting point. In researching Pollock's life, I discovered he was capable of being the man in the myths, but was also the man who read Rimbaud in translation, listened to jazz and loved to bake. I was drawn to curious facts: for instance that those powerful, fantastic hands were missing part of a right index finger, that the "drip" method had been associated with an obsession with urination (hence the critics' sobriquet "Jack the Dripper") and that among the appropriations of Pollock are Pollock dances, a JacksonPollockBar ashtray, a Pollock dress and a Pollock suit, musical compositions called Pollock Pieces and, of course, Pollock Poems.'

Series Editors' Biographies

Bronwyn Lea was born in Tasmania in 1969 and grew up in Queensland and Papua New Guinea. She studied Literature and Writing in California, where she lived for twelve years, and holds an MA in Creative Writing from the University of Queensland. She is the author of *Flight Animals* (UQP, 2001), which won the Wesley Michel Wright Prize for Poetry and the FAW Anne Elder Poetry Award. She lives in Brisbane with her daughter, Tia.

Dr Martin Duwell was born in England and has lived in Australia since 1957. He was a publisher of contemporary Australian poetry in the seventies and eighties and since that time has written widely on the subject in essays and reviews. He is the author of a set of interviews with poets, *A Possible Contemporary Poetry* (Makar, 1982) and, with R.M.W. Dixon, is the editor of two anthologies of Aboriginal song poetry, *The Honey-Ant Men's Love Song* (UQP, 1990) and *Little Eva at Moonlight Creek* (UQP, 1994). He has also edited an edition of the Selected Poems of John Blight and was one of the editors of the *Penguin New Literary History oif Australia* (Penguin, 1988). He has strong interests in medieval Icelandic literature and Persian language and literature.

JOURNALS WHERE THE POEMS FIRST APPEARED

The Australian, ed. Barry Hill. GPO Box 4245, Sydney, NSW 2001.

The Australian Book Review, ed. Peter Rose. PO Box 2320, Richmond South, VIC 3121.

Blue Dog: Australian Poetry, ed. Ron Pretty. c/o Poetry Australia. PO Box U34, Wollongong University, NSW 2500.

Eureka Street, poetry ed. Philip Harvey. PO Box 553, Richmond, VIC 3121.

Five Bells, ed. Anna Kerdijk Nicholson. Poets Union Inc. PO Box 91, Balmain, NSW 2041.

Heat, poetry ed. Lucy Dougan. School of Language and Media. University of Newcastle, Callaghan, NSW 2308.

Island, ed. Peter Owen. PO Box 210, Sandy Bay, TAS 7006.

Journal of Australian Studies: Creative Arts Review, ed. Richard Nile. Curtin University of Technology, GPO Box U1987, Perth, WA 6845.

Meanjin, poetry ed. Peter Minter. 131 Barry Street, Carlton, VIC 3053.

Quadrant, poetry ed. Les Murray. PO Box 82, Balmaine, NSW 2041.

Salt-lick New Poetry, ed. Clint Greagen, Luis Gonzlez-Serrano, Jeffrey Payton and Susan Paterson. 104 Rennie St, Coburg East, VIC 3058.

Southerly, ed. David Brookes. Department of English, Woolley Building A20, University of Sydney, NSW 2006.

The Sydney Morning Herald, poetry ed. Angela Bennie. GPO Box 506, Sydney, NSW 2001.

Westerly, eds. Delys Bird and Dennis Haskell. English, Communication and Cultural Studies, The University of Western Australia, Crawley, WA 6009.

ACKNOWLEDGMENTS

The general editors would like to thank Carol Hetherington for her research assistance with this book.

Grateful acknowledgment is made to the following publications from which the poems in this volume first appeared:

Robert Adamson, 'Flag-Tailed Bird of Paradise.' *Meanjin* 62. 3 (2003): 30.

Adam Aitken, 'At Batu Caves, Kuala Lumpur.' *Meanjin* 62. 4 (2003): 144–45.

Eric Beach, 'Wimmera Easter Sunday.' *Salt-lick New Poetry* (Winter, 2003).

Judith Beveridge, 'Appaloosa.' *Salt-lick New Poetry* (Autumn, 2003): 50.

Elizabeth Blackmore, 'Dog Bite.' *Blue Dog: Australian Poetry* 2.3 (2003): 14.

Janice Bostok, 'The Widow.' *Salt-lick New Poetry* (Spring, 2003): 20.

Peter Boyle and MTC Cronin, 'Objects of You in Water.' *Southerly* 62.3 (2002): 75–81.

Elizabeth Campbell, 'Letters to the Tremulous Hand.' *Blue Dog: Australian Poetry* 2.3 (2003): 45–6.

Lidija Cvetkovic, 'A Seed, a Crutch, a Heart.' *Heat* 6 NS (2003): 103–04.

Luke Davies, from 'Totem Poem.' *Heat* 6 NS (2003): 227–51.

Bruce Dawe, 'For Annie.' Southerly 62.3 (2003): 47.

Jan Dean, 'Signed Auguste Rodin.' *Blue Dog: Australian Poetry* 2.3 (2003): 40.

Tim Denoon, 'Clovelly.' *Island* 91 (Summer, 2002–3): 150.

Dan Disney, 'Ecce Hombre.' *Journal of Australian Studies* 77 (2002): 129–30.

Laurie Duggan, 'British Columbia Field Notes.' *Heat* 5 NS (2003): 22–9.

Chris Edwards, 'The Awful Truth.' *Australian Book Review* 250 (April, 2003): 45.

Liam Ferney, 'Angel.' *Southerly* 62.3 (2003): 22.

Kris Hemensley, 'The Happiness of Winter.' *Salt-lick New Poetry* (Autumn 2003): 30.

Rae Desmond Jones, 'El Niño.' *Meanjin* 62.3 (2003): 16–17.

Aileen Kelly, 'Mood / Tense.' *Blue Dog: Australian Poetry* 2.3 (2003): 14.

Emma Lew, 'Sugared Path.' *Meanjin* 62. 4 (2003): 115.

Kathryn Lomer, 'On the Tongue.' *Island* 93/94 (Winter/Spring, 2003): 216–18.

David Malouf, 'Out of Sight.' *Heat* 6 NS (2003): 52.

Kate Middleton, 'Your Feet / Love Poem.' *Australian Book Review* 248 (February, 2003): 34.

Graeme Miles, 'The Road in the Rear-View Mirror at Night.' *Blue Dog: Australian Poetry* 2.3 (2003): 38.

Les Murray, 'Through the Lattice Door.' *Quadrant* 47.3 (March, 2003): 24.

Ted Nielsen, 'Pax Romana.' *Meanjin* 62.2 (2003): 55–7.

Π.O., 'The Platypus.' *Heat* 6 NS (2003): 169–72.

Peter Rose, 'U-Bahn.' *Meanjin* 62.2 (2003): 58.

Brendan Ryan, 'The Paddock With the Big Tree In It.' *Island* 91 (Summer, 2002–3): 154.

Margaret Scott, 'Land.' *The Weekend Australian* 1–2 February 2003: 10.

Kerry Scuffins, 'Your House.' *Blue Dog: Australian Poetry* 1.2 (2003): 55.

Tom Shapcott, 'Totems.' *Blue Dog: Australian Poetry* 1.2 (2003): 47–48.

Maggie Shapley, 'Evidence.' *Westerly* 48 (2003): 124.

Ian C. Smith, 'Keys.' *Quadrant* 47.5 (May, 2003): 49.

Vivian Smith, 'Happiness.' *Heat* 6 NS (2003): 252.

Norman Talbot, 'Seven New South Wales Sonnet-Forms.' *Five Bells* 10.1 (2003): 27–28.

John Tranter, 'Bats.' *The Sydney Morning Herald* 16–17 August, 2003 Spectrum: 22.

Chris Wallace-Crabbe, 'Our Birth Is But a Sleep and a Forgetting.' *Eureka Street* 13.6 (July–August, 2003): 14.

Linda Weste, 'Heldentod.' *Salt-lick New Poetry* (Spring, 2003): 52.

THE JOSEPHINE ULRICK POETRY PRIZE 2005

The Josephine Ulrick and Win Schubert Foundation for the Arts
are the proud sponsors of Australia's richest prize for poetry.
It is named in memory of Josephine Ulrick
whose three great loves were art, literature and photography.

FIRST PRIZE IS $10,000
AWARDED TO A POEM OR SUITE OF POEMS UP TO
TWO HUNDRED LINES

For prize dates and conditions of entry contact:
Josephine Ulrick Poetry Prize 2005,
Attention Sonia Pucki,
School of Arts,
Gold Coast Campus Griffith University,
PMB 50, Gold Coast Mail Centre, Qld 9726, Australia

s.pucki@gu.edu.au
www.gu.edu.au/school/art/ulrick
ph. (07) 5552-8428

PREVIOUS WINNERS OF THE JOSEPHINE ULRICK POETRY PRIZE
2004: Nathan Shepherdson
2003: Judith Beveridge
2002: Judy Johnson
2001: Anthony Lawrence
2000: Kathryn Lomer
1999: Jean Kent

The winning entry for 2004 is printed below.

NATHAN SHEPHERDSON

I HAD A DREAM I WAS TALKING TO LAWRIE DAWS ON THE PHONE

we were talking about the marks made by a snake in the sand
movement weighed by scales of a different kind
of course time is also measured with wait
slow hands rummaging through a box of eyes
large hands that throw an ocean at the sun
still looking for the blind eye
the one we really see with
how_do_we place an eye in the landscape
place both our eyes in our hands
and look at ourselves
as if we were wet beneath the mercury on the mirror
our heads tuned like a silent radio of light
conception in the mind's male womb
images as still as the memory of a dead man
is colour too literal for words
words mixed with dirt and chromium full stops
raked across our souls
and watered by the mere fact that we breathe
strange isn't it..t
this single object that is your life
used memory stuffed into a bag made of clocks
every phrase supplied with a pair of ears

thought as a self portrait for listening
strange isn't it..t
this single object that is your head
this block of stone that fell from the sky
you spend your entire life
pushing it from one corner of the room to the next
tracing the marks on the floor
and calling it perspective
you refer to a dictionary of shadows
read aloud to the geologist god with teeth made of fire
philosophy should always be kept separate from its meaning
one word could always be one word too many
less than itself but equal to the sound it makes
lips are entitled to be red
entitled to consume bodies without names
entitled to nail vowels to the oldest living tree
does intelligent speech sleep under the tongue
can language be ground into a pigment
one more word could never be enough
no word is ever the same as itself
what is said is lost to the seconds it takes to say it
what is said replaces the air with no air
an absence born with gravity's face
the handles always bleed when the truth is passed around
the blood moulded into lipstick for demons
the handles always bleed when the truth is passed around
an instant truth

a type where the heads are ripped off the shoulders of
    question marks
and fed to coffee soaked dreams
buried beneath the spelling of a word like thought
the head you are thinking with is stolen
it remains the property of the next decision you will make
minute sketches kept frozen in saliva
anodised trays overflowing with unnumbered souls
visual aphorisms mobilised against synthetic space
plastic cups to catch the prophet's tears
limbless notions filmed with a hand held conscience
the head you are thinking with is stolen
it once belonged to a clown who wore death's clothes
his oversize shoes a baked black porcelain
he was seen walking away from another grave for laughter
the jokes in attendance were without mouths
gagged by an appetite for speech
what you understand and what you don't understand are the
    same thing
identical difference followed into its own (w)hole
as slow as the speed of light
which is quicker
the brushstroke ⟶ or the thought of the brushstroke
images as still as
    as still as
    as still as
    ⟶ a tongue on a plate
as still as the smell of mint in the hair

or the cold perfume in wet paint

provenance recites itself onto the studio wall

the dead colouring of stains that drip from a thousand blue
     nipples

a turpentine sleep is rubbed into the brow

callipers are used to measure the width of an artist's brain

to assess the extent of eidetic embalming

the prayer is broken by the praying

as you make the approach to the white window

lines remember how they are drawn

hard sung into the echoing imprimatura

umber

burning with the resonance of peeled oxygen

luce di sotto

the static theatre of flat surfaces

the answer is never solely alone with the question

form is both recognition and denial

an approach to what is left and a departure from what is made

each gesture is interrogated

cut open with the blade from an idea

the fur scrape of the brush

the microtonal lisp as the finger retreats from a new mark

all fingerprints inevitably magnify into a map for touch

how_does_a landscape live in its own head

how_do_you pull paint through its own pores

pull the eyelids away from the face with pliers

pull figures out of abstract waters with a gaff

reason is safe when it is not used

not called upon to refill the anatomy with sand
or be held responsible for the murder of details
imagine
one complete moment
a moment vacuumed of its physics
a moment from which the sound has been evacuated
a moment drenched in a poetry of conclusions
a man
a man sits in a chair
a bronze chair with a high back
it has the patina of a park statue
it is without ornamentation
and the man
he is not asleep he is not awake
so the colour of his eyes will never be known
it is as if he has been wiped over with his own soul
his body is naked and shaved
his skin is very white
glazed like the meniscus on a spoonful of milk
he has never left the chair
he will never leave the chair
worms regenerate beneath his feet
and the man and the chair are inside a glass cube
bare architecture built with emptied light
it attracts a pack of emaciated dogs
they are without eyes nor ears nor fur
they sniff the ground as if it were flesh
and the man and the chair and the cube

are fixed with the eroded veins of the mountains
volcanic cathedrals
encircled by the fossils of worshippers yet to be found
gargantuan punctuation
marked out in a sentence that reads the curve of the earth
strange isn't it..t
every Christmas another bar is unwrapped and put in place in
    the red cage
eventually it will house a jar that holds the last breath from
    Piero's lungs
from the ceiling will hang an egg on a chain
the prayer is broken by the praying
art is the dust lining the ventricles of an apple
history will never recognise its own shape
it pumps clouds into a room the size of a book
painting is to create violence without movement with
    movement
the sedimentary pink is perfectly bled into winter dusk
as you make ready to fit out the night in metaphysical skin
you look for the moments with broken bones
and gather the stones with bruising
you drop echoes into a well of silence
swallow the moon whole and digest your life